Think... bold blues

Gorgeous greens

Regal reds

Mellow yellows

COLOR!

Editor: Brian Kramer
Senior Associate Design Director: Ken Carlson
Project Editor and Writer: Jan Soults Walker
Contributing Art Director: Mary Pat Crowley
Contributing Writer: Kellie Kramer
Contributing Photographers: Pam Francis, Scott Little, Janet Mesic Mackie,
  T. Miyasaki, Jeff Noble, Alise O'Brien, Danny Piassick, William Stites, Rick Taylor,
  Paul Whicheloe (Anyway Productions Inc.)
Copy Chief: Terri Fredrickson
Copy and Production Editor: Victoria Forlini
Editorial Operations Manager: Karen Schirm
Managers, Book Production: Pam Kvitne, Marjorie J. Schenkelberg, Rick von Holdt
Contributing Copy Editor: Jane Woychick
Contributing Proofreaders: Sue Fetters, Sara Henderson, Heidi Johnson,
  Margaret Smith
Editorial and Design Assistants: Kaye Chabot, Karen McFadden, Mary Lee Gavin

Meredith₀ Books
Editor in Chief: Linda Raglan Cunningham
Design Director: Matt Strelecki
Executive Editor, Home Decorating and Design: Denise L. Caringer

Publisher: James D. Blume
Executive Director, Marketing: Jeffrey Myers
Executive Director, New Business Development: Todd M. Davis
Executive Director, Sales: Ken Zagor
Director, Operations: George A. Susral
Director, Production: Douglas M. Johnston
Business Director: Jim Leonard

Vice President and General Manager: Douglas J. Guendel

Meredith Publishing Group
President, Publishing Group: Stephen M. Lacy
Vice President-Publishing Director: Bob Mate

Meredith Corporation
Chairman and Chief Executive Officer: William T. Kerr

In Memoriam: E. T. Meredith III (1933–2003)

***Trading Spaces* Book Development Team**
Kathy Davidov, Executive Producer, TLC
Roger Marmet, General Manager, TLC
Tom Farrell, Executive Producer, Banyan Productions
Sharon M. Bennett, Senior Vice President, Strategic Partnerships & Licensing
Carol LeBlanc, Vice President, Marketing, Strategic Partnerships
Erica Jacobs Green, Publishing Manager
Elizabeth Bakacs, Creative Director, Strategic Partnerships

Trading Spaces

Spaces

COLOR!

Meredith® Books
Des Moines, Iowa

Trading
Spaces

contents

6 Introduction

Get acclimated to the world of color by taking the Color Attitude Quiz.

10 Let Yourself Go

Celebrate and express your individuality with fun and fresh decorating ideas for colorful, care-free spaces.

30 Meditate on This

Take a breather from the hectic pace of life. Explore soothing, reflective color ideas for serene spaces.

50 Grand Funk

It's time to get your groove on! Suss out daring, flashy style ideas for attention-grabbing spaces.

70 Warming Trend

Kick back, relax, and recharge with cozy, casual ideas guaranteed to warm any space.

90 Exotic Adventures

Pack your bags for a journey into the frontier of decorating. You'll bring back international style ideas for spaces with a world view.

104 Elegant Attitude

Hobnob among the decorating elite with these classic, refined decorating ideas for sophisticated spaces.

124 Energized with Accents

See that the difference truly is in the details. Inject lively, invigorating touches into your creative spaces.

144 Dramatic Finale

Take a bow and receive a standing ovation! Choose bold, passionate looks for show-stopping spaces.

158 Episode Guide

174 Index

Color It Cool

From the Paint Reveal segment at the start of the show to the unveiling of the finished rooms, COLOR is center stage in nearly every *Trading Spaces* episode, calling out to the homeowners and viewers at home, "Hey, look at me!"

Sure, you're already intimately familiar with the creative cast of *Trading Spaces*—the host, designers, and carpenters who help transform mere rooms into show-stopping spaces in only 48 hours. Still, there's one *Trading Spaces* character you probably haven't considered, and this character is the unsung hero of the show.

It's color. Color plays a variety of critical roles in many of the decorating plots the *Trading Spaces* designers hatch. Room color—potentially dozens in one space—is one of the most prominent features of any *Trading Spaces* episode.

Color is one of the top recommendations homeowners give the designers when they meet for the first time. The recommendation to add some color is quickly followed by the Paint Reveal segment, in which the designer opens cans of paint to squeals of joy or groans of displeasure. (If the relationship between homeowner and designer is going to derail, it usually happens right about the time the cans of paint are opened.)

Color is the tool *Trading Spaces* uses to unify a room quickly and inexpensively. Although it happens more often than is shown on television, the designers often ask homeowners to scour the home they're working in and pull together specifically colored items. For example, behind the scenes during Indiana: Fieldhurst Lane, Doug asked his homeowners to grab anything dark,

rich, and textured to finish off their bedroom makeover. Ten minutes later, homeowners returned with a yard sale's worth of unconventional, color-coordinated accessories, including wicker place mats, dusty yearbooks, and forgotten holiday decorations.

Color is usually the first thing homeowners react to during the final Reveal. Comparisons to dirty diapers or the set of *The Dating Game* have been memorable color reactions, but the overwhelming majority of homeowners are pleasantly surprised by the bold bursts of color.

Using This Book

Most decorating books about color start out with a lecture on color palettes or a science lesson about light waves and pigments. Not *Trading Spaces Color!* (OK, this book *does* have a few technical tidbits. But they're so cool that you'll end up using them to amaze other shoppers at the paint counter of your local home center!)

Each chapter in *Trading Spaces Color!* focuses on the end goal of decorating a room, because that's what *you're* focused on—the final result. Dozens of methods, techniques, and color palettes can help you warm or energize a room, encourage creativity, soothe the mind, release your inhibitions, or add a dignified air to a space.

Jump into any chapter that sounds like it can help fulfill your decorating desires. You'll find easy how-to advice, insider secrets, and inspiration and ideas from the creative *Trading Spaces* cast.

If you're not sure about your take on color, take the quiz that begins on the next page. It's fun and fast—and you just might learn a bit about your personal style and color preferences.

Get ready to color your world!

The Secret to Selecting Colors

Free yourself to change your mind about color. Repeatedly.

Cut yourself some slack. The *Trading Spaces* designers seem sure of their design choices on TV, but behind the scenes, they frequently change their minds . So can you. Sure, boldness is important when picking colors, but so is flexibility.

For example, Doug's color choice for the bedroom featured on page 72 was originally a deep gold, a shimmering shade of yellow that captured the warmth of a late-summer sunset. However, at the paint store, Doug suddenly decided he'd already "done a yellow room" while in Indianapolis (his infamous "Back from Brazil" foot-centric living room featured on page 64) and needed to change his plans.

Doug compared a bushel basket of harvest tones with his original color choice and eventually selected a shade of orange with similar intensity and richness. (Over the course of the episode, the theme, like the color of the room, was fluid: "Indian Harvest," "Autumn Harvest," and "Autumn Sunset" were all titles the *Trading Spaces* designer used to describe the warm fall palette of the room.)

In the end, the real point of the color became clear: The right shade of yellow can soothe your soul after a long day, but so can the right shade of orange (or blue or green, for that matter). Know what mood or effect you want a room to create, and then stay open-minded and flexible until you discover a color that does the job.

What's Your Color Attitude?

Find out how you really feel about color with this handy-dandy Color Attitude Quiz. Read and answer each of the following 15 questions to learn a bit more about color—and yourself.

1. My idea of the perfect Saturday night out would be:

a. Enjoying drinks at an art gallery before attending the opening performance of a new symphony.

b. Savoring a steak dinner and then watching the latest Tom Hanks movie.

c. Slurping a bowl of Thai noodles and watching skits performed by an improvisational comedy troupe.

d. Taking a stroll on the beach, followed by conversation around an open fire.

e. Sharing pizza and sandwiches with friends at a neighborhood bar and grill.

2. I'll see any movie that features the following actors:

a. Ruppert Everett or Julianne Moore.

b. Harrison Ford or Julia Roberts.

c. Benicio del Toro or Parker Posey.

d. Brad Pitt or Meg Ryan.

e. George Clooney or Sandra Bullock.

3. If the *Trading Spaces* crew were to make over a room in my home, I'd want:

a. My bedroom styled with a combination of steel, chrome, and leather accessories.

b. My kitchen redone in a crisp blue and white scheme with new tile countertops and decorative molding.

c. My bedroom transformed into an exotic oasis with rich tapestries, unusual woods, and bold colors.

d. My dining room overhauled to include distressed furniture and a photo collage wall with photocopied pictures of my friends and family.

e. My family room warmed up with walls painted in harvest colors, piles of pillows, and comfy seating.

4. Red may be the color of passion, but the red that gets my engines revving is:

a.

b.

c.

d.

e.

5. For Halloween, I'd like to dress up as:

a. A beauty queen.

b. A vampire.

c. A tube of toothpaste.

d. A fairy princess.

e. A sheriff from the Old West.

6. The *Trading Spaces* designer I'd most like to go to lunch with is:

a. Hildi.

b. Vern.

c. Doug.

d. Gen.

e. Frank.

7. The colors I'd most like to see combined in my bedroom would be:

a.

b.

c.

d.

e.

8. A great color combo for my living room would be:

a.

b.

c.

d.

e.

9. If I had a free round-trip ticket to anywhere in the world, I'd visit:

a. Paris (for Fashion Week, of course).

b. New York City.

c. Indonesia, to tour ancient mosques and temples.

d. Jamaica.

e. The Grand Canyon.

9

10. The *Trading Spaces* designer I would *never* let in my house is:

a. Frank.

b. Kia.

c. Edward.

d. Vern.

e. Laurie.

11. The first thing I want people to see when they enter the house of my dreams would be:

a. A signed contemporary oil painting hanging on the wall.

b. A console table with a brass lamp and a place for resting the mail.

c. A one-of-a-kind wire and scrap metal sculpture/chandelier.

d. An antique garden urn brimming with ferns and ivy.

e. An oak coat tree and hat rack.

12. I wouldn't be caught dead wearing:

a. Overalls, flannel shirts, or sneakers.

b. Hawaiian prints, miniskirts, or platform shoes.

c. Button-down shirts or khakis.

d. A gray business suit.

e. A tuxedo or a formal dress with crinoline .

13. The one luxury item I'd take on a desert island would be:

a. My razor.

b. Shampoo.

c. A set of watercolors.

d. My journal.

e. My pillow.

14. Something you'll *never* find in my house is:

a. Wicker anything.

b. Inflatable furniture.

c. Matching pieces of bedroom furniture.

d. Leather and chrome.

e. Queen Anne legs.

15. My ideal kitchen would include:

a. Teak cabinets, chrome hardware, concrete countertops, and lots of skylights.

b. Stained cherry cabinets, granite countertops, gold faucets, and numerous pendent lights.

c. Open stainless-steel shelving, butcher-block work surfaces, and industrial-style appliances.

d. Whitewashed pine cabinets, gauzy curtains, and an indoor herb garden.

e. Warm oak cabinets, display areas for my collectibles, and stools and benches for family and friends to hang out on.

To score this amazingly scientific quiz:

Tally the number of times you answered a, b, c, d, or e in the quiz. The letter you chose most frequently indicates your general decorating, design, and color attitudes, as listed in the chart below.

If you answered: This is your attitude:

a. Chic	You've got style and you like to show it, whether spare and minimal or sleek and stunning. Color should be neutral and subtly blended, with bold, show-stopping accents that "pop" when you look at a room.
b. Classic	You know a good thing when you see it! You gravitate toward traditional styles (with a few twists, of course). You want to furnish your home with looks and colors that can last a lifetime, adding new accessories and decorative touches along the way. Look for regal, luxurious colors.
c. Funky	As in other areas of your life, you'll try anything in your home decor. You look for unusual materials and exotic influences. Color is fun and feisty for you—with lots of contrasts.
d. Romantic	You want your home to take you away from the hustle and pressures of life. You strive to add personal, intimate touches to your home and furniture. Your colors are soft, soothing, and relaxing.
e. Casual	For you, comfort is paramount. You want to look good, but not by sacrificing any comfort. Warm, easy color that envelopes your soul and no-fuss neutrals are just what the color doctor ordered.

If your answers are spread out between several options, you may have an eclectic style, built around mixing and matching the looks and items you love. Who knows? You may be on your way to creating an entirely new style for the 21st century.

LET YOURSELF GO

Chapter 1: Let Yourself Go Are those preconceived notions about color you're carrying? For a moment, imagine life with carnival colors and jelly bean hues. Then set aside the rules that say these playful palettes are off-limits in your house and get ready to discover how wonderful a room can feel once you let yourself go...

One for the Records

COLOR LESSON: Confidently combine color with a dash of black.
BACKGROUND: Motivated by a splashy swath of fabric, Hildi totes in stacks of vinyl records and yards of punchy fabric. The colorful record labels make a dramatic impact as they repeat across the wall while new slipcovers play up the fun, fruity palette.

Play It Again ◀

The decorating inspiration for one room often comes from blending multiple ideas and materials. For Hildi, a bandanna-like square of fabric (see page 15) sporting lemon yellow, raspberry, and teal hues with black accents shared a surprisingly similar color palette to a $60 stack of vinyl record albums from a thrift store. Could the assorted colors on the record labels serve as small pieces of do-it-yourself artwork? Absolutely! Arranged on one wall in a neat gridlike pattern, the album labels offer pleasing punches of random color encircled in broad bands of black. Lightweight items such as these record albums can be secured to walls using screws, a glue gun, or hook-and-loop tape.

Colorful Cover-Ups ▼

With the color palette in place, Hildi moved on to the furniture. Plain plywood boxes become stylish when painted in bold party hues. Rather than stacking, these multicolored caches built by Ty line up side by side, holding stereo speakers and equipment and underlining the wall treatment.

Hildi, whom Paige refers to as "the Slipcover Queen," stitched all the colorful cover-ups herself to complement the bandanna hues and rejuvenate the existing furniture. Assorted throw pillows play up the palette and make the room more inviting. If your pillows have seen better days, you can slipcover them easily too.

To learn how to measure for ready-made slipcovers, turn to page 68. Turn to page 142 to see how easy it is to sew simple pillows.

Before ⌶01:42:22.14

The owners of this living room say they've "always had country." They want "happy and warm," and it's OK to re-cover the furniture.

13

Reflecting on the Theme ◄

Dozens of one type of object can't help but make a statement, and the mirror hanging on an opposing wall multiplies the effect of the record-album wall art. The simple black frame allows it to fit into any setting, and this works particularly well because the frame echoes the look of the black vinyl record albums.

Panel Discussion ◄

Color has the power to entice the eye, so use it to create interest and draw attention. At the picture window, for example, bands of teal blue flank a frothy length of white sheer fabric, creating a soft look that balances the visual weight of the black accents. The pretty curtain panels, which thread onto the rod, are easy to make, especially when you begin with a single fabric. Also, teal reappears as a pillow on the sofa and again as a free-flowing stripe on the wood panel screen nearby. *Discover easy ways to create your own screen on page 136. See how to sew (or no-sew!) a simple rod pocket and panel on page 48.*

Paint Packs a Powerful Punch ◄

Four paint colors—yellow, teal, orange, and purple—instantly bring drama to the walls for little money. However, paint may not offer the most comfortable and durable results on upholstered furniture. Disenchanted with the plaid fabric on one of the homeowner's favorite chairs, Hildi nixed the idea of sewing yet another slipcover and instead spray-painted the chair black. Painted-on flowers provide a flourish. (The homeowner was a good sport about the transformation.) *For tips on choosing and using brushes and rollers, turn to page 36.*

Inspiration Incorporation ▼

To finish the room, Hildi put the bandanna that initially inspired her design under the glass top of a coffee table. Whether your inspiration is artwork, dinnerware, fabric, or some other object, consider including it in the room to emphasize your color theme.

Gain Color Courage

COLORING LESSONS

When the Wizard gave the Lion a medal in *The Wizard of Oz*, our feline friend gained courage. You already have what it takes to invite color into your home—the *desire* to make your rooms lively and livable. That craving, supported with some basic color principles, is really all you need to gain color courage.

✱ **Know thyself.** Love is what makes any relationship long-lasting, so don't welcome "the color of the moment" into your home unless you truly love it. If you're not certain which colors are your true loves, take the quiz on page 8. If you're torn between two or more hues, let the color wheel on page 21 give you some insight about how color works.

✱ **Seek inspiration.** Flip through magazines and books. Watch *Trading Spaces*. Visit home shows, home centers, and open houses. Take notes, make copies, and snap pictures whenever you see color used in ways that capture your attention and make you smile. Then build on those ideas to create a palette that pleases your eye.

✱ **Welcome change.** After you peg your palette, start adding color in ways that are easy to change. A gallon of latex paint costs little; and painting a few walls, a ceiling, or a piece of furniture requires only an afternoon. Adding a colorful decorative accent piece is another low-cost option.

✱ **Small doses.** If you're not accustomed to living with color, begin with a few accessories, such as a colorful pillow or two. Gradually add more color sources—artwork, frames, and lampshades, for example—as your courage blossoms.

✱ **Be bold.** As you realize successful results, your courage flourishes. Now you can begin investing in colorful room elements, such as rugs, upholstered furniture, window treatments, and slipcovers.

An Illuminating Idea ◀

Hildi's funky lamp consists of a drilled length of PVC atop an MDF (medium-density fiberboard) base that's painted white. Simple lamps like this one can be illuminated with a small bulb and socket base or with a night-light assembly—both are available at home centers and lighting stores. To wire a more traditional-style base-and-socket-type lamp, purchase a lamp-wiring kit from a home center or lighting store and follow the directions *below*.

Make a Lamp out of Anything
Get ready to exclaim "Let there be light!"

You can transform all kinds of vessels—from vases and jars to vintage boxes and old boots—into lamps. The following basic steps are all you need to know:

1 **Drill a hole,** from top to bottom, through the vessel or object. If you have access to a drill press, the task will be easier. Ask someone at a home center if you need a special bit for the material you're drilling through to avoid damage.

2 **Purchase a lamp-wiring kit,** available at a home center or lighting store. The kit should contain a standard threaded rod, washers, and a harp holder. Lighting stores offer specialized parts that you may need, such as spacers, finials, and decorative bases.

3 **Stack the lamp components,** including the socket and harp, and measure from the bottom of the socket to the bottom of the lamp base; this is the preliminary rod height. Add only enough to allow the rod to screw into the bottom of the socket and subtract enough so that the bottom of the rod will recess ¼ inch into the bottom of the base. (Drill a 1-inch-wide and ½-inch-deep recessed area in the underside of the base, if needed, to allow the lamp base to sit flat.) Use a hacksaw to cut a standard threaded rod to this measurement.

4 **Decide where the cord** can exit the lamp base. If the base has feet, leave the cord loose; otherwise drill an exit hole in the back of the lamp base.

5 **Insert the rod** through the lamp base. Use a washer to secure the rod to the base. Thread the electrical cord through the rod. Screw the rod through the harp holder and into the bottom portion of the metal socket; then securely tighten the connections. Carefully pull apart a few inches of the top end of the cord to separate the two wires

(A); tie the wires into an underwriters knot (B). Strip off about ¾ inch of the plastic covering at the ends of the wires and attach the bare wires beneath the socket screws (C) with a screwdriver. Add a plug to the other end of the cord.

6 **Attach the harp,** insert a bulb into the socket, and then test it.

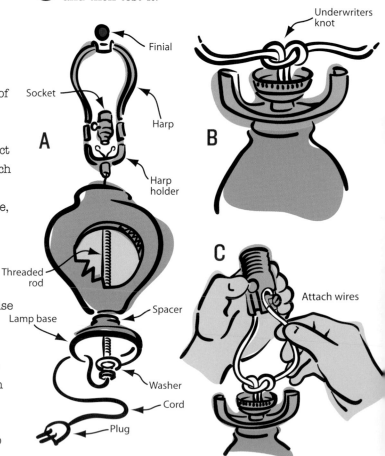

Just as some things are worth saying again, you can create visual impact in any room by decorating with multiples of an object. Check out these other repeating themes from the *Trading Spaces* archives.

Give little things big impact. Several small objects grouped together can make a strong statement and serve as an attractive focal point. Hildi demonstrated this in Providence: Phillips Street by hanging several silver zeros together to cover a large portion of a living room wall.

Add spice with slight variations. Change the height of each item by placing some on shelves, add a small touch of one color in different shades to the same item, or set a few items askew. Doug employed this variation trick in Austin: Wycliff when he installed a clock wall and set each clock to a different time zone.

Keep it simple. Install simple decorative objects easily. For example, use a 2×4 shelf for a row of votives or wood wall pegs to show off a vintage hat collection. This spirit was behind Gen's choice to attach botanical postcard copies to a wall using lowly stickpins in Maple Glen: Fiedler Road.

Watch for opportunities. Consider the potential of multiples on the floor, tabletops, mantels, door frames, drawer fronts, windows, or even the ceiling. When redecorating a living room in Providence: Phillips Street, Vern affixed several small red-frame mirrors to the ceiling around a hanging light fixture.

Use more than one group. Repeating simple items can be part of the signature style of a room. Choose three or four small items to repeat throughout the room. In Wake Forest: Rodney Bay, Vern repeated square white shelves, candlesticks, and African violets in a romantic bedroom.

Before

Sure, white in a kitchen looks clean, but it's also b-o-r-i-n-g! Someone needs to lavish this place with color—and quick.

Contempo-ribbean Kitchen

COLOR LESSON: Look to a favorite item for color courage.
**BACKGROUND: White plastic laminate cabinets were blank canvases
waiting for Doug and crew to paint a masterpiece. The contemporary
four-color palette mimics a sunny day in the Bahamas. Moldings boost the
tropical character quotient too, and open shelving offers stylish storage.**

Color and the Candlestick ◄

The owner of this plain kitchen adored the feisty colors of the
candlestick shown prominently on the countertop. Ultimately, Doug
adopted the kicky combination of bright red, sunny yellow, rich
burgundy, and muted green and used it to transform a stale
collection of all-white, flat-faced plastic laminate cabinets. Lemon-
lime walls set off the bold color scheme.

Doors Galore ▼

This makeover could have been introduced as
"Two days, $1,000, and 40 doors and
drawers." That's how many pieces of
cabinetry Doug and the homeowners had to
remove, sand, prime, and paint tomato red.
Narrow moldings, cut and finish-nailed with a
nail gun to the cabinet faces, provide an
opportunity to play up the additional colors
in the palette. Doors and exposed cabinet
sides feature concentric bands of molding
in yellow, burgundy, and green. Drawer
fronts feature yellow lengths of molding
bordered in green. The original black
countertops and appliances offer a fitting foil
for the bright hues.

   Of course, the six-panel interior door
couldn't remain untouched. The neighbors
painted it red to match.

Flowery Finish ▼

Adding a bundle of vibrant birds-of-paradise
in a yellow vase is the perfect finishing touch
for this kitchen abloom in happy colors.

19

Open-Minded Thinking ▲

Leaving some of the doors off the upper and lower kitchen cabinets opened up stylish new storage options. For these sections, interiors were painted red. Simple baskets on the exposed shelves store everything from linens to produce. Baskets offer portability too, so you can use them to transport the contents to wherever it's needed.

20
··

In the Spotlight ▲

A blocky fluorescent light fixture went bye-bye, thank goodness. This sleek and sexy chrome-and-blue beauty (bought for less than $100!) deserves a spotlight of its own. Space above the upper cabinets didn't go unnoticed either: Doug put it to work displaying pottery pieces in rich blue and green.

Stylish Steel ▲

The existing stainless-steel sink and the owner's beautiful chrome dinette set with fun multicolor seat cushions (see page 18) made brushed chrome pulls a smart choice to further freshen the cabinet doors and drawers. They offer complementary glimmer to this glamorous redo.

....21

COLORING LESSONS

Take a Spin on the Color Wheel

Round out your knowledge of color with these basics.

A color wheel comprises 12 hues: three primary colors, three secondaries, and six tertiary colors. Color relationships built on these color groups form the basis of color theory in design. Any combo of colors can work successfully together—after all, success is in the eye of the beholder—but understanding the color wheel makes playing with color all the more fun.

Primary. Red, blue, and yellow are the primary hues. These colors are pure: You can't create them from other colors, and all other colors are created from them.

Secondary. Orange, green, and violet are secondary hues. They land midway between the primaries on the color wheel; they're formed by combining equal portions of two primary colors.

Tertiary. Mixing a primary color with the secondary colors closest to it creates a tertiary color. Red and orange, for example, make an orange-red color, blue and green make a green-blue, and so on. Tertiary hues are less vivid than secondaries.

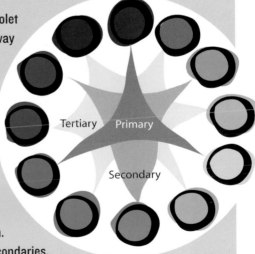

Molding Character ▶

To obtain the rich red hue on the cabinetry, the neighbors had to apply four or five coats of paint. This covered all the pink-tinted primer and helped them achieve a smooth finish. The nail holes in the moldings could have been filled and touched up with paint, but everyone agreed that the distressed look was too cool to cover up. Take a look at the tips below for another way to achieve a weathered finish on new (or old) surfaces.

Painting Furniture and Cabinets

Transform ordinary or has-been pieces with a few creative strokes. Whether clean and crisp or aged and antiqued is your style, paint is the fast ticket to a customized look.

One of the quickest ways to fire up the look of kitchen cabinets is to paint them. Follow these steps for great results. The strategies work for both laminate and wood cabinets as well as for wood furniture.

1 Clean surfaces with TSP (trisodium phosphate), a cleaning agent available at home centers and hardware stores. Wear rubber gloves and eye protection as you work. Rinse well and let dry.

2 Lightly sand the surfaces and wipe clean with a tack cloth. Paint on high-quality primer. If you're going to finish with a dark color, use primer tinted with the finish color. Let dry.

3 Lightly sand the primed surface if the grain is raised. Wipe clean with a tack cloth. Brush, roll, or spray on the finish color. Apply as many coats as needed to achieve rich, uninterrupted color; allow each coat to dry according to the manufacturer's directions before applying the next coat. For kitchen cabinets, choose semigloss or high-gloss paint for an easy-to-clean finish that will stand up to wear and tear. (See "Liquid Assets," page 35.) Latex paints emit the least odor in a confined space.

Distressing Deeds

Even the newest piece looks old when you try this faux-finishing technique:

A Sand and prime the piece. Let dry. Apply the desired base color. Let dry.

B Rub candle wax over the base coat, going with the grain and applying the wax only where natural wear might occur, such as on edges and around handles.

C Apply the top coat of color; let dry. Sand the top coat wherever you applied wax to distress. If desired, repeat waxing, painting, and sanding for a third color. Wipe the surface with a tack cloth and then seal with two coats of clear satin-finish polyurethane.

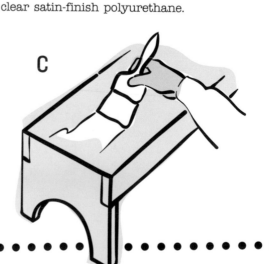

A Stable of Tables

The most versatile piece of furniture in your living room? Forget about the sofa and look to the coffee table for a textbook lesson on how to combine form and function beautifully.

Roughing it. You may think of coffee tables as a sign of refinement, but they don't have to be. Tables can be made to fit any decor, be it funky, casual, or just different. Gen's coffee table for a Georgia O'Keeffe-influenced living room in San Diego featured firewood legs for a nonfussy, totally rustic look.

Make a play space. Coffee tables are a fantastic place for kids of any age to work on projects, create art, or play games. Creative table designs might include built-in containers for toys, art supplies, and more. Vern added a removable mini-sandbox to a simple white coffee table in Nazareth: First Street.

Leggy looks make the difference. If you love the top of a table but abhor its legs, update those gams. Home centers and hardware stores carry a large selection of unpainted wooden legs, or you can fashion legs yourself. Doug filled large plastic tumblers with plaster and rebar and attached them to a kidney-shape table in a retro living room in Washington, D.C.: Cleveland Park.

Tray chic. If floor space is at a premium, choose a coffee table that's collapsible or removable, depending on your needs for floor space. Vern used two circular metal trays on folding legs as temporary coffee tables in a Portland living room that occasionally serves as a guest room.

It's the tops. Think of your coffee table top as a canvas with legs. Paint, embellish, and enhance as you would a piece of wall art. In Seattle: 56th Place, Hildi painted a curvy magenta stripe across a coffee table for graphic effect.

23

24

This master bedroom was architecturally beautiful, but it lacked the spunk and playful eclecticism that the homeowners employed elsewhere in the house. Though they asked for an "oasis of serenity," Frank has a hunch they'll be happier with something more fun.

Before

A Bold Kiss

I could be wrong on this, but I don't think the homeowner wants serene.

COLOR LESSON: Try daring color anywhere.
BACKGROUND: Frank explores the "palette-able" possibilities in a sedate master bedroom. By giving the room a lavish kiss of color, coupled with some tongue-in-cheek sculptures, storage solutions, and wall sketches, this room celebrates individuality and banishes formerly humdrum style.

Face the Facts ◄

To unify this fun-loving space, Frank focused his design around a playful face theme. Eyes fabricated from flexible copper tubing (bent to follow a kraft paper pattern) peer out from an orange wall that's punctuated with plump crimson silk lips. To make a padded headboard like this sexy number, cut plywood to the desired shape (the upper and lower lip shapes were cut separately here), wrap the plywood in acrylic batting and fabric, and then staple the material to the back of the plywood. Decorative pillows lend more color and softness to the bed; one central pillow playfully features an appliqué of a glamourous gal with flowing hair.

Adding another fun and fluffy flourish are lamps topped with lavender tulle and whimsical paper crowns. The lamps sit atop matching end tables flanking the platform bed, which was custom-made for the episode.

More vibrant personality comes into play from a collection of hats and hatboxes on display. The hats and boxes rest on white metal shelf brackets. In a move that added sunny contrast, Frank splashed bright yellow throughout the room, including the vinyl chairs topped with red cushions.

To learn how to apply appliqués to pillows, turn to page 88.

Picture This ◄

A portrait of the homeowners' daughters inspired Frank's bold palette. Soft shades of purple and a green inset help distinguish the fireplace wall from the other walls, which are tall, warm, and orange. To create the gauzy purple look, the homeowners first rolled on light purple paint. With this coat still wet, they used a second roller to lightly apply a layer of medium purple; then they blended the two hues with a sponge.

Hanging the painting above the fireplace helps bring all the colors together on one focal-point wall. To introduce the all-important doses of red to this end of the room, Frank chose crimson paint for the storage cabinet and a hope chest. Black and white stripes around the top and bottom of the chest add nice, crisp detail. *For tips on painting and distressing furniture, see page 22. For tips on choosing and using brushes and rollers, turn to page 36.*

RED is for passion. Whenever you want to give a room a little zing, red is the color of choice. It's not so surprising, of course, if you think about how red oozes drama. It is the color of anger, of blood, of love. Use it when you want to convey passion.

Care to See Some Etchings? ▶

For a final fashion-forward touch to this whimsical room, Frank and the neighbors freehand painted a faux sketchbook of lovely ladies in the latest runway styles. Thinned gray paint enhances the illusion. For added dimension and a dash of whimsy, a 12-foot dowel, whittled at one end to a point, was painted to look like a pencil. Frank also glued paintbrushes to the wall above the hatbox storage display, creating a playfully artistic design (see page 24).

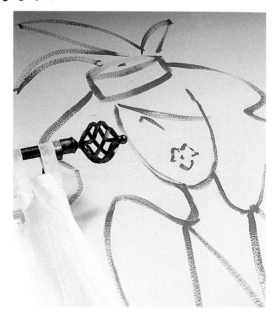

Coding Lessons

Coming to Terms with Color

You'll amaze your friends by knowing these definitions of common color terminology, and you may impress yourself when you use this knowledge to make bold, creative palette decisions for your decor.

✳ **Analogous.** Colors next to one another on the color wheel are said to be analogous, or related (you know, like color kin). Perhaps it's their neighborly, side-by-side location. But no matter how you pair analogous colors, they always seem to get along.

✳ **Complementary.** Complementary colors sit directly opposite each other on the color wheel. Despite resting on opposite sides of the fence, these colors can look smashing when paired; each increases the intensity of the other.

✳ **Hue.** Think of this as a nickname for "color"—the only difference is that hue refers to a whole clan of color, such as greens; no matter how the greens are tinted (with white or shaded with black), they are all still the same hue.

✳ **Intensity.** When you refer to how bright (or dull) a color is, you are describing its intensity, or chroma. Colors in their purest form are most intense. Adding gray to colors turns the intensity down. Apple green is a high-intensity color while dusty sage is a low-intensity hue.

✳ **Monochromatic.** Though a monochromatic scheme has only one color, it's far from boring. For wonderful variations in a single color, add black or white or tint the base color with a complementary color.

✳ **Neutrals.** Take color out of the equation and you're left with the tried-and-true neutrals: black, white, and gray. Mix these around a bit and you come up with shades of taupe, sand, tan, and beige, to name only a few. However you label them, neutrals seem to work with any accent color you choose.

✳ **Primary.** Remember in preschool how you learned to mix colors to make other colors? The colors that you started with— red, blue, and yellow—are known as the primary colors. They're pure and cannot be created by mixing other colors.

✳ **Secondary.** Back to the preschool lesson again: Mixing equal parts of two primary colors yields a secondary color. Red and yellow make orange, blue and yellow make green, and blue and red make purple. Take a look at the color wheel on page 21 and notice that the secondary colors are located between the primary colors used to create them. When you mix unequal parts of two primary colors, you create a variation of the true secondary hue.

✳ **Shade.** Mixing black with any hue creates a "shade" of color.

✳ **Spectrum.** Have you ever held a prism up to the light? The rainbow of color that you see shooting out to the walls, ceiling, and floor is known as a spectrum.

✳ **Tint.** Toss white into a hue and you end up with a "tint."

✳ **Tone.** Tints or shades may also be called "tones." Sky and wedgwood are tones of blue.

✳ **Triadic.** Draw a triangle with equal sides in the center of a color wheel so the triangle points fall on three colors. These three colors, which are spaced equidistantly on the color wheel, make up a triadic color scheme. If you decide on a triadic scheme, make one color dominant and use the other two as accents.

Be Image Conscious

Use this nifty gadget to re-create professional-looking artwork and other images on the wall.

Murals, painted on walls and ceilings, have long been a favorite for bringing color into a room. If the thought of painting anything freehand makes you nervous, consider investing in a crafts-quality opaque projector. These projectors, which are available at crafts and art stores for less than $50, allow you to project an enlarged version of a selected image onto the wall (or another surface). You can then trace the outline and fill it in with paint.

When hunting for images, consider fabric swatches, art books, personal photographs, CD cases, calendars, catalogs, greeting cards, wrapping paper, and any other inspiring object that catches your eye. If you have an artistic bend, draw your own small-scale masterpiece and use a projector to enlarge the piece to mural size.

Follow the manufacturer's directions for casting the image onto the wall and enlarge it to the desired size. The projector can reproduce phrases and words on a wall as well. Use a sharp pencil to trace the image; then paint as desired or use markers or paint pens. You may also paint the image while it's still projected onto the wall to more closely match the colors. Or use colored pencils to outline sections of the image in the appropriate hues and then use the outlines as reminders when choosing paint colors.

28

Get Inspired!

Surprise yourself with outrageous color palette inspiration sources.

You'll find fantastic color and style ideas aplenty when you open your eyes to the world around you. The *Trading Spaces* designers have been spurred on by a gaggle of goofy things, and some of the following just might serve as your starting point too.

What about your favorite accessory? Take almost anything to your local hardware store or home center, and they can likely match the shade. (Hold still, Fido, and let the nice man scan your fur.) Gen matched the walls in an Austin living room to the large poster hanging above the fireplace.

Have you looked at the world around you? Look to nature or your environment for endless color possibilities. Autumn leaves or the brick on your neighbor's house can be translated into paint colors. In a Philadelphia dining room, Laurie took inspiration from the way the sunlight shone against rust and black buildings.

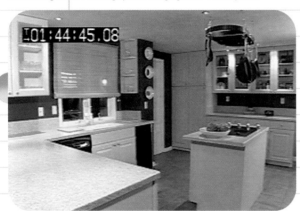

Have you peeked in the refrigerator? Some of the most beautiful and vibrant colors are in the crisper. Paint colors inspired by fruits and vegetables can give your room a bold yet natural feel. Using artichoke hearts for inspiration, Gen painted a kitchen with shades of green, white, and purple in Colorado: Berry Avenue.

Did you look in the mirror? Fashion and home decorating aren't all that different. Get inspiration from your fanciest dress, your favorite pair of shoes, or those bling-bling earrings you love so much. In Long Island: Split Rock Road, Gen matched kitchen paint colors to the sea glass necklace the homeowner loved to wear.

What about the packaging? Marketing execs spend countless hours designing packaging for your favorite things. Make use of their expertise by cribbing the color combos they choose. In a Washington, D.C., bedroom, Hildi used the unmistakable Tiffany & Co. color combination of teal, white, and silver.

MEDITATE ON THIS

Chapter 2: Meditate On This

Color is a powerful tool that creates fun and excitement or soothes and calms. The good news is that you're not limited to pastels when you want tranquillity. Take a moment to reflect on how color works to make the following settings as serene and peaceful as a mountain stream.

32

Polynesian Retreat

My inspiration came from the homeowners' love of Hawaii.

COLOR LESSON: Combine earthy hues, subtle texture, and tranquil tropical overtones to soothe.
BACKGROUND: Gen added romance to this master bedroom with a casual Polynesian vibe. Muted natural hues and breezy mosquito netting make it seem as if the beach is right outside the window.

Neutrals for Napping ◄

Earth tones and natural texture ground any room in comfort. As the starting point for this island fantasy, Gen fashioned a bedspread from an almost retro-style fabric featuring rows of leaflike shapes in khaki, sand, and rusty orange on a cream-color background. Playing on the darkest tone in the fabric, the once-white walls and ceiling take on the restful attire of dark taupe.

An orangey hue Gen calls "a kind of sandy sun color" unifies the existing wood furniture and the tropical theme. New knobs add a punch of dark contrast to enliven the furniture makeover.

Standing in as an island-style headboard is a plywood rectangle gussied up with a piece of grass cloth that's topped with a triple-pane wood frame. Staining the wood frame before securing it to the grass cloth keeps the look clean. For stability, a headboard like this one can be nailed to a horizontal 1× board that's level and screwed to wall studs. *For tips on painting furniture, see page 22.*

Soothing Touches ►

Greenery promises to refresh any room, and adding a tropical palm to this private retreat is a smart touch that enhances the faraway feeling. Matchstick blinds, softened with a simple sheer valance that's threaded onto a rod complement the texture of the headboard. The black iron candle sconce provides a romantic glow.

Canine pals Lucky and Murphy weren't overlooked during the makeover—after all, this is their bedroom too. Gen stitched two dog beds using leftover fabric and even added elegant cursive monograms for each dog.

Before
01:42:57.19

The homeowners call their bedroom a "blank canvas," and they're ready to say goodbye to the "flowers and pine." They want the room to be as cozy for them as it is for their faithful pooches.

Gracious Getaway ▲

Of course, no tropical getaway worth its salt comes without a gauzy mosquito net canopy. Gen fashioned this one from airy yards of white tulle. To draw the eye upward and to allow the tulle to drape gracefully around the bed, the fabric is stapled to a small rectangular frame that's screwed to the ceiling and painted to seamlessly blend in. The effect is simultaneously romantic and earthy, dreamy and adventurous.

Painting an existing wall mirror dark brown makes the mirror a natural companion to the stained headboard frame. As a bonus, the mirror multiplies the effect of sunlight coming into the room, making the space seem more refreshing.

Large square pillows in sunflower and earthy brown increase the color quota in the room and work with the canopy to make the bed a soft and inviting refuge.

Square pillows are easy to make. To learn how, turn to page 142.

34

More Earthy Elements ◄

Chic paper lampshades on all the light fixtures provide texture that works well with the grass-cloth headboard and matchstick blinds. The addition of these creamy hues ensures that the space remains a place for slumber without feeling overly dark.

For artwork, Gen had the neighbors paint plain canvases with colors gleaned from the makeover. Masking tape makes it easy to create the clean background lines, and the abstract designs are no-holds-barred freehand renditions. Because they're free-form, making a "mistake" is virtually impossible.

COLORING LESSONS

Liquid Assets

There's gold in "them thar" buckets— and green and blue and red...

Paint offers one of the easiest, most cost-effective ways to transform a room with color. Choosing the type of paint you need is one of your first decisions. For help in selecting hues, turn to page 47.

Quality Counts

Buy the best paint that you can afford for a room; you'll likely end up with a product that's durable and easy to apply. One coat should yield beautiful results. You may need to experiment with different brands until you find one that offers all these noble qualities for a price you can live with.

Oil Versus Latex

Paint comes in two main types—oil-base (also called alkyd) and water-base (known as latex).

Oil-base paint stands up well in high-use areas (such as on cabinetry, doors, and trim, and children's play areas), and it doesn't show brush marks. Oil-base paint tends to give off strong odors, can be messy to clean up—you'll need turpentine or mineral spirits—and is known to yellow over time. Some of the ingredients in oil-base paints have been singled out as pollutants. Keep oil-base paints separate from the regular trash, and take them to sites that accept toxic materials.

Latex paint gives off less odor than oil-base paint, cleans up with water, and dries quickly (though this can result in visible brush marks). Latex paints are appropriate for almost every application, and some high-quality water-base formulas resist wear as well as oil-base paints do. Dispose

of water-base paints by letting the paint dry out, then throwing the can into the garbage.

Sheen Chic

Paint promises more than a rainbow of colors: It has a variety of sheens as well. Here's a look:

✱ **Flat paint** offers a dull finish that does a great job of concealing wall imperfections. Because it doesn't clean well, however, use flat paint only in low-activity areas, such as living and dining rooms and bedrooms, and on ceilings.

✱ **Satin or eggshell** provides subtle luster and is easier to clean than flat paint. It's a suitable choice for busier areas such as hallways and children's bedrooms.

✱ **Semigloss** works well in areas where you want more cleanability, such as in playrooms, kitchens, and bathrooms. Because it is shinier and more reflective than satin, it doesn't hide flaws on the walls.

✱ **High-gloss,** not surprisingly, offers the highest shine of all. Because it tends to be a durable finish, it is a popular choice for creating lacquer-look furnishings and for painting trim. If you consider it for walls, keep in mind that it will actually highlight any imperfections, so it is best limited to small areas.

Brush up on these basics when it is time to buy brushes and rollers for your next paint job. Then follow the painting tips for professional results.

What to Buy

If you plan to use latex paint, choose brushes with synthetic or nylon bristles that aren't flagged (meaning split) which can cause the finish to foam. The metal band around the bristles (called a ferrule) won't rust if it's stainless steel or copper.

When using oil-base paints, select long, supple natural China bristles, which are black or white hog hairs; choose either flagged or tapered. Natural bristles will frizz if you expose them to water-base paint.

Like quality paint, a high-quality brush will give you good results and last a long time.

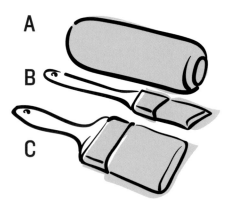

Look at the illustration, *above*. A high-quality roller cover (A) is worth the price. To check quality, spread the nap apart; if you can't see the cardboard core, it's dense enough to deliver a smooth coat of paint. Select a shorter nap when painting smoother surfaces and choose longer naps for rougher surfaces.

Tapered sash brushes (B) have long, thin handles you hold like a pencil. Small sizes are especially handy for painting narrow areas of windows, doors, and molding. A 1½-inch brush and a 2½-inch brush will get you through most paint jobs.

A 2½- or 3-inch flat brush (C) will help you cut in at corners and around windows and doors.

Painting Walls and Ceilings

1 **Scrape off loose paint,** patch holes, and sand rough areas. Clean surfaces with water and a mild household detergent; rinse and let dry. Use primer when painting surfaces that are stained; also use it over colors that are darker than the new color you've chosen and on walls that were once covered with wallpaper. Using quick-release painter's tape, mask off trim; with drop cloths, cover other features that you don't want painted, such as furniture and floors.

2 **Cut in with a brush** (see illustration, *below*). Apply a swath of paint along the perimeter of the walls and ceiling. These are the areas the roller can't reach.

3 **Roll on paint.** Using a roller with an extension handle lets you reach the tops of the walls without a ladder. Depending on the length of the extension handle and the height of your room, you may need a ladder to paint the ceiling. Saturate the roller by rolling it in a paint-filled tray and using the ridges in the tray to roll off excess. Starting in an upper corner of the wall, apply the paint in N- or M-shape strokes and work from top to bottom and left to right. Move the roller horizontally in 8- to 9-square-foot sections (about 2×4 feet) to even out the paint; work back into the wet edge of the previous area. To remove roller marks and even out the texture, use light up-and-down strokes, pulling up at the end of each stroke to reduce, or feather, the edge. Allow paint to dry according to manufacturer's directions.

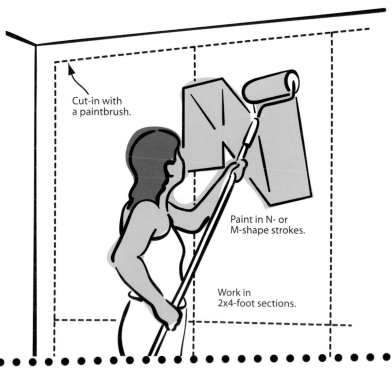

Cut-in with a paintbrush.

Paint in N- or M-shape strokes.

Work in 2x4-foot sections.

Sleep on It

Wake up to some new ideas: Make your bed more than just a mattress on a frame.

This sampling of creative—and sometimes colorful—sleeping arrangements proves that adding a mosquito net canopy is only one of many ways to make a bed the dramatic focal point in your bedroom.

Go natural. Stain or oil an unfinished wood bed to keep the natural grain visible. Stains come in many varieties, from wood tones to primary colors, while maintaining a natural look in a room. In Chicago: Spaulding Avenue, Hildi chose to oil a large wood-frame bed, enhancing its deep purple-brown color.

Use nontraditional materials. Have an open mind when exploring the home store aisles. Plumbing conduit can make a canopy frame, large molding can serve as side slats, or roof flashing can become a headboard. Doug used PVC pipes to create a four-poster bed in North Carolina: Southerby Drive.

Make it part of the architecture. Think of your bed as part of the room itself, not merely as a piece of furniture. Build the bed into the wall or raise it on a built-in platform with stairs. Gen's Moroccan-inspired bed in Boston: Ashfield Street attached to both the floor and ceiling, adding architectural details to the room.

Double the function. Why not create built-in storage space under the bed frame? Be creative with the size and style of drawer fronts and knob pulls to personalize the piece. In London: Garden Flat, Gen designed a bed with two large drawers on either side of the frame to make up for the homeowner's lack of closet space.

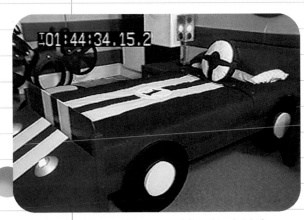

Make it life-size. Make kids' dreams come true by making their beds resemble favorite things. Fairy tale castles, sailboats, and tree houses can inspire a new theme bed. Vern's room in Long Island featured a race car bed complete with striped linens and working headlights.

Tranquil Horizon

Vern uses a true-blue solution to revitalize a bland bedroom.

COLOR LESSON: Choose blue to soothe and rejuvenate.
BACKGROUND: A bevy of blues and elegant touches of black mix to make a master bedroom retreat that's both restful and stylish. The room also offers a geometry lesson with its painted stripes and plywood squares.

Don't Be Blue—Choose Blue ◄

Too bad blue has gotten a bum rap from its association with down days. Studies show it's a wonderful color in an adult bedroom because blue is so calming it can lower blood pressure. Vern deftly uses this misunderstood shade—with gray touches and some black accents—in a paint color he aptly dubs "ocean." (Think of how tranquil you feel watching rhythmic ocean waves rolling ashore.) Vern makes the room cozier by mixing in deeper blues—with lush dark blue velvet serving as a sexy new cover for a chair. The velvet also appears as curtain panels and as stripes on the bedding and pillows.

Plywood Dresses Up ▼

Who knew ordinary ¼-inch plywood could be so gorgeous? Vern cleverly uses 1-foot, 11-inch squares of the material to give the wall behind the bed an unexpected touch of architecture. Staining the squares transparent blue allows the grain to show, and alternating the direction of the grain for each panel creates subtle pattern. *To learn an easy way to attach squares like these to a wall,* *turn to page 82.*

Before

In this master bedroom, Vern and the homeowners agree that the brown and white can take a hike. The space needs a focal point too, and Vern's paneled wall is a perfect strategy.

39

> **"I wanted this room to be gender-friendly, which I think blue is,"** Vern says. **"I wanted this to be a balance of him and her, and blue is such a calm and relaxing color. I especially love the blue velvet.**

Classic Black ▲

Black will always be a classic color, so it's hard to go wrong injecting it in small doses in a room. In this bedroom, Vern gave an ordinary four-poster bed, a chest of drawers, and bedside tables an elegant new air by painting them black. Silver pulls on the storage pieces and garlands of glass beads on the bedposts act as "jewelry," accessories that add sparkle. Lighting sconces create an additional glow.

40 Strategically Striped ▶

Any room can easily earn its stripes—check out the technique on page 42.

Running stripes horizontally rather than vertically can help make a high-ceilinged room seem more intimate; it also creates a contemporary look. Vern uses horizontal stripes in this master bedroom to continue the palette of blues and to lure attention *around* the room, away from the ceiling.

Because the vertical posts of the bed do encourage an upward glance, glass bead garlands adorn the pendent fixture, giving it a look that's as finished and finessed as the rest of the room.

A trio of white vases, along with white candles in black iron pendent holders, keep the area above the doorway from appearing empty.

Ceilings: White or a Color?

The *Trading Spaces* designers often opt for color on the ceiling. Light colors can make a ceiling seem higher, but what fun is there in plain old white? Many designers tint ordinary white paint with some of the wall color to help the ceiling seem more a part of the palette; others decide on a contrasting or a related hue. Choose what works for you: If you want a room to appear more intimate, select a darker shade to create the illusion of a lower ceiling. A lighter shade makes the ceiling seem to recede and evokes a brighter look for the room.

Stripes on the Horizon
Turn traditional thinking on its side with stripes stretching across the wall, not down.

The only tools you need to paint horizontal stripes: a measuring tape, a pencil, a carpenter's level, quick-release painter's tape, and a narrow roller.

1 Use painter's tape to tape off the ceiling and trim. Choose three shades of any color and roll on the lightest shade as the base coat. Let dry. Decide how wide you want the stripes; then use a measuring tape and a pencil to mark the height of each stripe on the wall.

2 Use a level and pencil to extend the marks horizontally around the room. If you want, use a colored pencil that corresponds to the color that the stripe will be.

3 Tape off each stripe with painter's tape. Run your thumbnail along the edge of the tape to prevent the paint from bleeding underneath. (Some painters use an artist's brush to apply clear glaze along the outer edges of the tape. Once dry, the glaze creates a tighter seal.)

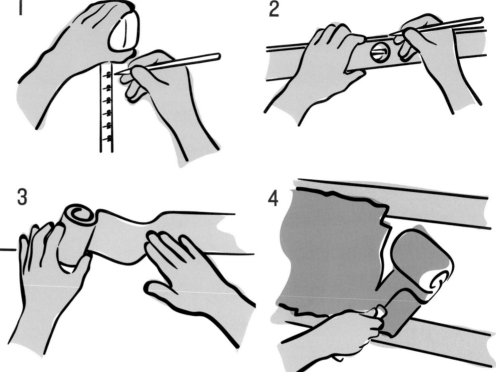

4 Use a roller to fill in the colors of the stripes. Before the paint dries, remove the tape. If you wait until the paint dries, some of the color may peel up with the tape. If this happens, though, the bald spots can be easily fixed with paint and a brush.

42 Stripes don't have to run horizontally. Use a weighted string or a plumb bob to measure off perfectly straight vertical stripes. Or get creative and use a straightedge and measuring tape to create diagonal designs.

A Brush with Beauty

Freshen up fast with a perfect paint treatment.

There seems to be no end to the great looks you can create with paint, and the *Trading Spaces* crew proves the point time and again...

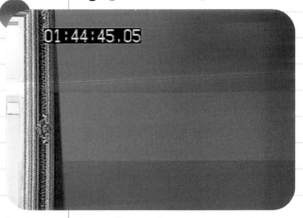

`01:44:45.05`

Use sheen to your advantage. When you choose your paint color, give some thought to its finish. Use the same paint color with different levels of sheen, such as a satin and a gloss, to create a subtle effect on your walls. This is how Hildi chose to finish off a dining room in Alpharetta: Providence Oaks.

`01:40:28.02`

Project a specific image. Do what schoolteachers have done for years—use an overhead projector (or an opaque projector) to trace an enlarged image onto your walls. After you trace the design, use small artist's brushes to fill in the design with your chosen palette. Doug's chinoiserie walls in an Asian-inspired bedroom in North Carolina: Southerby Drive are a good example of this technique. For tips on projecting and painting images, see page 28.

`01:43:48.19.2`

Tape off geometric shapes. Use low-tack painter's tape to mark off stripes, squares, rectangles, or other shapes. After you paint inside the tape shapes or over various taped lines, remove the tape before the paint dries. In Quakertown: Quakers Way, Hildi used this technique to create her infamous orthogonal design in a basement family room.

`01:41:54.07`

Freehand your own design. Let your creativity flow by painting any type of pattern designed with any number of colors. Get inspiration from your own garden, vintage postcards, or your favorite artist. Laurie created a Matisse-inspired mural in a basement family room in New Jersey: Tall Pines Drive.

`01:39:45.10.2`

Blend colors right on the wall. Select three shades of the same color. Brush each color onto the wall in random, alternating patterns. Switch colors and blend the edges to create a soft, mottled color wash. In California: Dusty Trail, Doug blended three shades of blue in a calming bedroom.

Before

`401:42:40.27`

The homeowners say they already have a living room where they can sit and talk. They want this to be a gathering space where they can relax and watch TV. Facing off with the big-screen TV, Gen rises to the challenge and makes it work.

Souped-Up Digs

COLOR LESSON: Use color for balance.
BACKGROUND: A bowl of Thai soup inspired
the savory palette for this Washington, D.C., family
room. Gen used clever color tricks to integrate a huge-screen TV into
the space, while playing up a simple and elegant Asian-style theme.

Bowled Over by Balanced Color ◄

The flavorful color palette suggested by a bowl of soup
helped Gen strike a beautiful balance between
technology and Asian refinement. Gen's favorite Thai
soup (which she playfully had delivered to the set)
featured a creamy coconut broth and a dash of cilantro
green. Mushrooms may have been missing, but that
didn't stop her from introducing a handsome light
mushroom hue for the walls. Creating Asian simplicity,
Gen traded out the existing ceiling fixture for a pair of
delicate lotus-blossom shades in soft white. Refreshing
lemongrass yellow accents completed the palette for a
family room that the homeowners use for watching TV
and relaxing with friends.

The Block Buster ▼

With the palette in place, Gen's most significant
challenge was dealing with an enormous big-screen TV.
Blocks of color—in a shade lighter than the base coat—
stand out behind the television as well as behind the
sofa. "By creating these boxes on the wall," Gen says,
"I was trying to de-emphasize the TV."

The block theme continues in the form of two cube-
shape rattan footrests, which can also hold beverages
or serve as makeshift seats when extra guests come
over to watch the big game.

The creamy coconut hue appears in the upholstery
for a 2×4-foot custom-made ottoman,
which offers yet more seating options.

45

Uncomplicated Style ▲

A sleek, custom-made sofa built by Ty replaces the original chunky seating because the "very, very simple lines balance out the big-screen TV," Gen says. Creamy coconut-color fabric unifies the sofa and the ottoman. Warm, dark stain highlights the arms and base of the sofa; the built-in side tables feature a clear coat for a pleasing variety of wood tones. An assortment of pillows add a bright punch of color and pattern.

Choose Your Hues

Selecting paint color from one little chip can be daunting. Study these tips and get your palette right the first time around.

Pick the paint color last.

It's wise NOT to choose your paint color first. Instead, take a cue from the *Trading Spaces* crew and let something in the room inspire the hue—fabric or a rug, for example. Start your room makeover with the most expensive or hardest-to-match piece; then work down to paint, which is inexpensive and can be matched to anything.

Vary the match.

Matching a paint shade to your inspirational piece is usually easy, but finding the same shade isn't that important; in fact, it's possible to overdo the matching business. Add lighter and darker versions of your chosen color to avoid a predictable look. The colors will blend together well as long as they share the same undertone, or intensity of dark or light.

Sleuth some color clues.

If you're still having trouble deciding on a palette, look at the clothing in your closet. The colors you wear are generally the colors you're most drawn to. Watch *Trading Spaces* and flip through decorating magazines to see what color combinations appeal to you and to discover some classic color palettes that have passed the test of time.

Consider goals.

Think about the mood you want to create in the room, how you want color to influence the size of the space, and where the room is located in the house. How you plan to use the room will influence your color choices: A high-activity space can handle high-intensity primary colors; a quiet bedroom would do well with calm colors. If you want the room to seem cozier, select warm colors, such as reds, oranges, or yellows. Make a room seem larger with cool hues, such as greens or blues.

Narrow the choices.

Go through a sampling of color cards and chips at home and refine the choices. Instead of comparing paint chip to paint chip, compare the color to something in your home. When you get down to a few choices, test the colors using the strategy on page 87 and make your final choice. Remember that choosing a paint color isn't a major life decision; if you ultimately aren't satisfied with your selection, repainting is always an option.

47

An abundance of sheer fabric at the windows offers softness to balance out the contemporary, linear lines of the sofa.

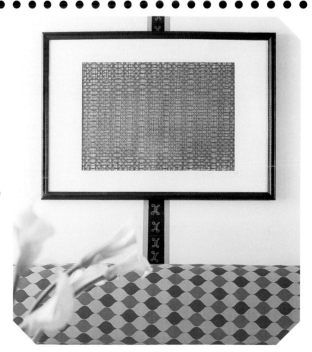

Fabric Focal Points ▶

Colorful fabrics create two important focal points in the room: a bold bolster for the sofa and framed artwork above the sofa. Notice how the block of color behind the artwork (see page 44) offers its own artistic input, as does the narrow brown stripe edged and decorated with lemongrass accents.

Breezy Beauty ◀

Tone-on-tone silk sheers layered over patterned lemongrass-color fabric play an important role at the windows, allowing light to filter in and cast a pleasing golden glow about the room.

Sew (or No-Sew) Rod Pocket Panels

Some of the best-dressed windows are wearing simple treatments—treatments you can make—whether you like to sew or not.

If you enjoy basic sewing, use your sewing machine to make this simple rod pocket panel. If needle-and-thread isn't your thing, then secure the rod pocket and hems by pressing the fabric under and securing the folds with fusible webbing (available in fabric and crafts stores). Use a hot iron to activate the webbing, following the manufacturer's directions.

To determine the length of the fabric piece, measure from the top of the installed curtain rod to the floor (if you plan a floor-length panel). Add 12 inches to this measurement to allow for the rod pocket and hems. For fullness in a two-panel treatment, start each panel with fabric that's as wide as the window. For a single-panel treatment, multiply the width of the window by two. Use the illustration as a guide for hems and the rod pocket.

Edgestitch 1/4" from second fold to form top of rod pocket.

Turn over 1/4" then 1 1/2"; edgestitch near first fold to form bottom of rod pocket.

Edgestitch hem.

Turn under 1 1/2" twice.

For a quick no-sew window treatment, attach clip-on curtain rings to the top of a piece of fabric and thread the rings onto a rod. If you don't want to hem fabric, use a twin-size flat sheet or a vintage tablecloth or table runner.

Everyday Art

Artwork for your home doesn't have to be expensive or require hours of effort. These ideas show how easy it is to bring framed visual bonuses into any room.

Check out the home store. When shopping at your local home store, keep an eye out for anything that would look great in a frame. Wire screening on a colored background, paint chips, and washers are all fun ideas. Doug framed strips of wood veneer to complete his makeover of a New York bedroom.

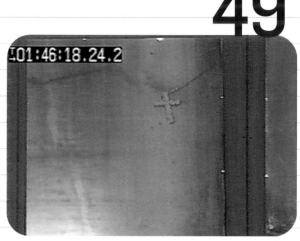

Think beyond photos. Add a personal touch to your room by displaying painted handprints made by your kids or having members of your family draw pictures of each other in their own unique style. Hildi left a little of herself in a living room in California: Peralta Street by photocopying parts of her body.

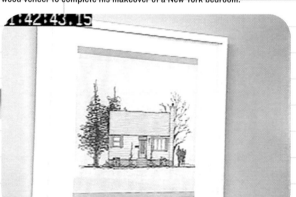

Revisit your plans. Frame copies of the blueprints of your home. Display garden plans or graphed furniture layouts. The look is unique and shows off the effort that went into creating the plans. In New Jersey: Lafayette Street, Vern framed an architectural drawing he created of the homeowners' house.

Dig through your closets. Give old items a second life by displaying them on the wall. Old textiles, illustrations from a used cookbook, or outdated maps gain interest when framed. Gen framed the old Scrabble board that inspired her Philadelphia basement rec room.

Take a walk around the block. Pressed flowers or found feathers look great when displayed. Even larger items like stones or shells can be hung in shadow box frames. In a bedroom in Boston: Institute Road, Doug hung several framed leaves he found while exploring the area around his homeowners' neighborhood.

Chapter 3: Grand Funk If you're the type of person who loves to raise a few eyebrows (think edgy fashions, wild candy colors, VW Beetles, and the Las Vegas strip), you may already be experimenting with the wild side of color. If not, this chapter may entice you to splurge with funky color schemes.

50

GRAND FUNK

Primary Election

Basic colors become fresh and funky with Hildi's help.

COLOR LESSON: Tweak a primary palette for a grand effect.
BACKGROUND: Hildi took color cues from a vivid abstract painting for this family room, combining bright orange, bold purple, rich ruby red, cobalt blue, even a checkerboard floor and a columned TV niche to create a family room as fun and flashy as its Las Vegas location.

Before

White walls, rose pink carpet, and 1980s pink couches left this family room a little pale. The homeowner also wanted something done with a gaping pass-through in one wall.

Red, Blue, and a Dash of Funk Too ◀

The colors in this abstract painting that Hildi brought from Paris inspired the fun palette in this family room. Ordinary primary hues are pumped up, so regular red becomes ruby and basic blue becomes indigo. Mounted in a frame spray-painted gold, the painting garners focal-point status above a bench that was originally an old sofa table. With a coat of gold spray paint and a cushion upholstered in "notice me" yellow-green, the bench adds another punch of slightly tweaked primary color.

Grand Opening ▲

With the original rose pink carpet out the door, Hildi repeated the checkerboard pattern from the painting, using playful orange and tan linoleum tiles on the floor. Deep burgundy paint for the walls and passionate periwinkle blue for the ceiling work together to give the room an enveloping aura.

Rather than close off a pass-through to another room, Hildi relocated the television to the opening. Burgundy draperies give the area a fitting theatrical feel; stately columns, painted burgundy to match the walls, reflect the architecture suggested in the painting. Glaze gives the ceiling a softer, cloudy effect—like a night sky.

53

End Table Transformation ▲

Two old end tables, with generous storage cabinets below, gain colorful cushioned tops and are pushed back-to-back to serve as an impromptu coffee table/ottoman. When guests arrive, these ottomans can serve as additional seating or as tabletops for refreshments or games.

One More Time Around ▲

A sofa and a chaise with fabulous clean shapes—from a thrift store—repeat even more colors from the painting, thanks to new tightly tailored slipcovers in fuchsia cotton and cobalt blue velvet. Pillows in black and bright orange kick this room up the color scale even further. Burgundy felt draperies dress the windows and make DVD viewing a pleasure any time of day.

Color Quiz: What Hues Are You?

Ready to find out what colors you can live with? Are you bold and sassy? Suave and subtle? Or something in between? Grab a pencil, stroll down memory lane, and take this color quiz. Then tally up your answers to see what color type represents the real you.

When you were in kindergarten, what finger paint colors did you grab first?

a. All the brightest hues—orange, red, yellow, blue—and you applied them with abandon. You even loved the look of the colors on your fingers. In your artistic creations, you didn't want to muddy the waters and concentrated on keeping the colors bright and beautiful.

b. You went for the primary colors but always made sure you had some white and black on hand to tone things down. By second grade, kids came to you to ask how to whip up the coolest colors.

c. Finger paints? You avoided them because they were messy. You used them a few times but couldn't get excited about the results. You liked watercolor paints, though, and were fascinated by the soft transparent hues against the textured paper.

At last, Mom and Dad say you can decorate your own room. You:

a. Head for the department store to find that Peter Maxx poster. It's the ideal beginning for the hip space you have in mind. You wonder how Mom will react to purple on the walls.

b. Wonder if it's possible to design a room around The Moody Blues' "Nights in White Satin."

c. Pull out your old denim jeans and decide to make them into pillows. Taking a cue from that soft, faded fabric, you want your room to be comfortable and stylish.

Your "dream" first car would have been:

a. A really fast, really red 'Vette, of course.

b. A midnight blue pickup, because it would have been as sharp-looking as it was practical—you could pile your friends in the back for a trip to the park to toss a Frisbee.

c. An import in classic black with tan leather seats.

Your prom dress/tux was:

a. Covered in flashy sequins and no one else at the dance had anything like it.

b. Silk from head to toe.

c. Tailored and drop-dead gorgeous.

After graduating from college, you travel to:

a. Vegas, baby, Vegas.

b. London and Paris.

c. Palm Springs.

Now you mostly shop for clothes:

a. At any vintage clothing boutique.

b. At a combination of places—online, in some of the trendiest boutiques, and at Banana Republic.

c. At The Gap.

Mostly A's: Go for the bold. You are definitely full of color courage and you're never afraid to open a can of paint and start redecorating.

Mostly B's: Splash some colorful artwork, pillows, and accessories in with your classic, mostly neutral furnishings—all upholstered in comfortable, touchable fabrics.

Mostly C's: Keep your surroundings low-key and classic and you're comfy and content. You prefer subtle, restful tones to bold, shocking colors.

55

Hip to Be Square

Lay vinyl or carpet tiles for underfoot color and enjoy gridlock for the first time.

Vinyl or carpet tiles are one of the more affordable ways to finish a floor with color, especially if you do the job yourself. Covering a floor with adhesive-backed tile is an easy project to complete in a weekend. Mixing tile colors within a checkerboard design or other simple pattern enables you to create quick custom looks. Here are some basics:

1 Make a clean start. Check that the wood subfloor or concrete slab is clean and free of debris. Remove all baseboards from the perimeter of the room.

2 Gather supplies. To allow for waste, purchase more tiles than the square footage of your room requires. For vinyl tiles, open the boxes in the room and let the tiles adjust to the indoor temperature overnight. You'll need a sharp utility knife with plenty of extra blades, a measuring tape, a carpenter's square, chalk line, and kneepads. Also, if the vinyl or carpet tiles you purchase aren't adhesive-backed, purchase the adhesive recommended by the manufacturer; take steps to ensure that your work area is well-ventilated. To apply adhesives, you also need to purchase a medium-size notched trowel.

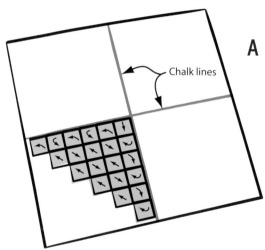

Chalk lines

A

3 Start with a plan. Read the manufacturer's installation directions and follow them carefully. Find the center of the room and dry-lay a row of tiles across the room. If perimeter tiles will have to be cut to less than half a tile, adjust the row slightly left or right in order to increase the size of the tiles that will be cut to fit around the perimeter of the room. Mark one edge of one of the center tiles in the row; use the mark as a guide for snapping two chalk lines to divide the room into fourths, or quadrants, as shown (A). Use a carpenter's square to align the marks so the chalk lines are square.

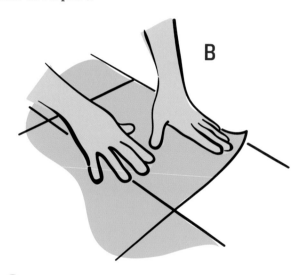

B

4 Place and press. Working in one quadrant at a time, align one corner of the first tile where the chalk lines intersect. The arrows on the illustration (A) indicate where to lay the first and subsequent tiles. Note that vinyl tiles have an arrow on the back of each tile. As you lay the tiles, make sure that the arrows on the backs all point in the same direction. This ensures a consistent pattern. Finish the entire quadrant before moving on to the next one. Use a straightedge and a utility knife to cut tiles for the perimeter of the room. For more-complicated cuts, make a pattern out of paper or cardboard and trace the outline on the tile; before tracing or cutting, check that the arrow on the tile back is pointing in the direction you want it to.

Make this job go even faster by inviting three friends over for a "floor party." Provide snacks and drinks while each person takes a quadrant, and before you know it, the job is finished. Take turns doing projects in each other's homes.

Tile Style

Whether you choose ceramic, carpet, or vinyl, here's plenty of proof that it's hip to be square.

Tiles have great color potential to offer, and practically no surface is off-limits. These *Trading Spaces* tile tactics will help you launch ideas of your own.

Add curves and colors. Covering your floor with one type of vinyl tile yields a unified look, but dare to do more: Use different tiles to create a checkerboard or stripes. Vern cut black and white tiles to fit together in a soccer ball shape in a boy's bedroom in New Orleans.

Be reflective. Use mirrored tiles to give your room an elegant look. Home centers and glass stores stock them in various sizes with or without beveled edges. Combine types and sizes to create a custom look. In Washington, D.C.: Quebec Place, Vern created a mirrored wall to add glamour to a bedroom vanity.

Save some cash. Vinyl floor tiles come in a multitude of styles and textures, including faux marble, faux stone, and ceramic imitations. Substituting tile for the real thing can give your pocketbook a break. In New Jersey: Lincroft, Laurie used faux-wood vinyl tiles instead of real wood parquet in a kitchen, creating a high-end look with a low-end budget.

Make your own. Ceramic tiles come in a variety of colors and styles, but you may want to take a different approach: Wearing gloves and safety goggles, you can break thrift store dishes with a mallet or tile nippers, and use the pieces in a one-of-a-kind design. Gen used this technique on a kitchen backsplash in Austin: Wing Road.

Create an illusion. Take careful measurements, find the center of the room, place your first tile, and build out from there. Try experimenting beyond the standard rectangle. Vern helped a living room look larger by placing carpet tiles in a diagonal pattern in Plano: Bent Horn Court.

COLOR LESSON: Choose deep colors for drama.
BACKGROUND: Edward chose supersaturated shades of purple, blue, and tomato red—along with shiny chrome accents and some shockingly bright snowboards—to decorate a fashionable, funky house for two college-age guys.

That's Deep, Man ◄

The velvety purple on the walls required equally rich color choices for the trim, accents, and fabrics. The oversize roxy red baseboard vibrates with attitude. Shiny chrome-frame furnishings and lush violet cushions set the stage for the electric green lava lamp and a pair of snowboards. Their splashy designs made them too cool to tuck away, so Edward propped them up on a sleek black shelf and deemed them art.

Intense Fellowship ▼

Employing contrasting colors in a room creates a setting that's intense and exciting—probably not a look for a bedroom. Vibrant purple and bright red are a striking choice in this space where the guys gather with friends for fun. Pairing two contrasting hues intensifies both of them. Look at the red slipcovered bench in front of the purple, red, and black wall design. The red and purple almost throb with color-saturated intensity. Edward found the glass coffee table, which nearly floats within a sea of color, for a mere $30 at a thrift store.

59

PURPLE is said to suppress appetites, but with college-age guys? Not! Used in this context, purple is all about having fun and living life to the fullest.

Add Glimmer with Metals

Metals of every kind can add new dimension to your color palette, and shiny silver isn't the only game in town. Rich copper, elegant bronze, glittering gold, stainless steel, and aluminum are a few of the metal finishes you can include in your decorating plan. You don't have to blow the budget on the real thing; check the paint department at crafts and home stores to find everything from hammered-metal spray paints to metal leaf products you can apply to all kinds of surfaces. Shiny finishes typically show fingerprints, so if you have lots of youngsters at your house, you may want to look for finishes that hide fingerprints, such as brushed chrome and stainless steel, or age-worn bronze and copper.

60

Seeing Red ◄

Red walls and fabric panels earn this college corner an A+. The cloud-shape wood countertop, spray-painted to shine like silver, is mounted on metal tubing atop a basic black MDF base that zigzags through space. Small low-voltage puck lights shine downward from beneath the tabletop. Four chrome-leg stools sport purple cushions to continue the passionate palette. Rather than paint stripes on the wall, Edward mounted black-painted 1× boards behind the bar and tacked on funky strips of flashing.

Wow Power ◄

Brilliant birds-of-paradise bring gusto to the bar area. Two small candles set on small silver dishes balance the display.

61

To land some shiny chrome furniture of your own, watch for going-out-of-business sales at restaurants, department stores, or bowling alleys. Also check the want ads and keep an eye out at flea markets.

Metal flashing is primarily used as a roofing component, but it's finding its way inside homes as material for creative decorating. Flashing is typically sold in rolls of varying widths. Cut it to the size and shape you want using a quality pair of sharp tin snips so that you can avoid crimping the edges. Always wear heavy gloves when cutting flashing (A) and watch out for the sharp edges when you're finished.

Secure flashing strips to horizontal or vertical surfaces with small finishing nails or brads (B), or use construction adhesive. Be forewarned: The latter method makes the flashing semipermanent!

Check out the home center for other metal products that might lend themselves to decorating. Patterned sheet metal, for example, has punched-out designs and is typically used to conceal radiators and heating vents. It comes in a variety of finishes, is sold in sheets, and is sturdier than flashing, so it's ideal for use as cabinet door panel insets or custom speaker cabinets. It can even be cut into a shapely valance.

Metal fabricators can create metal "skins" for tabletops, shelves, and even refrigerator fronts. Take the exact dimensions of the surface you want to cover, including thickness, and give these measurements to the fabricator. To cover an oddly shaped surface, make a template from kraft paper, cardboard, or newspaper.

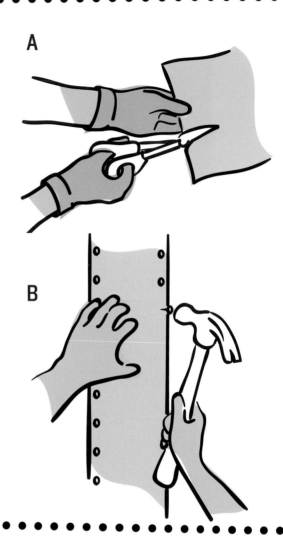

A

B

When you shape metal, always use the proper tools. The final results, like Edward's sculpture, can be stunning.

Edgy Art

Splashy, flashy, or just plain trashy—only you can decide what's really art...

Check out some of the offbeat items the *Trading Spaces* designers have used as one-of-a-kind artwork.

Keep track of time. Rather than buy a clock for a room, create your own. Battery-operated clock hands can be purchased at crafts stores or through online suppliers; what they point at is limited only by your imagination. In a romantic bedroom in New York: Sherwood Drive, Vern designed a large clock with candle sconces in place of numbers.

Move the outdoors in. Flowerpots and wicker aren't the only outdoor items that can update your favorite room. Think big as Doug did in Knoxville: Stubbs Bluff, where he spray-painted a shovel and pitchfork white and hung them on the wall in a country kitchen.

Sweeten the deal. Take a trip to the grocery store and shop the candy aisle. Decorating with your favorite sweet treats makes your mouth water and gives your room a carefree look. Hildi framed three types of candy in acrylic shadow box frames to add a fun touch to a basement room in Quakertown: Quakers Way.

Become part of the art. Add the ultimate personal design touch without using photos. Hang starched clothing items on the wall or make a plaster cast of a family member's foot. Hildi fashioned an elegant copper mesh bust of herself for a bedroom in San Diego: Elm Ridge.

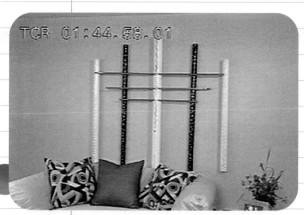

Bring your work home with you. Does a family member work with interesting materials for a living? Use those materials as accents. Frank created a pipe sculpture to pay homage to the homeowner's career as an electrician.

Barefoot in Brazil

You know, I bet you that foot stays!

COLOR LESSON: Let fabric inspire your palette.
BACKGROUND: Fresh from a jaunt to South America, Doug found inspiration in a bright, flowery sarong and swirly tie-dye fabrics he bought in Brazil. The international color palette impacted the walls and furnishings—as well as the homeowner's foot phobia.

Tie-Dye to Die For ◄

Though Doug traveled abroad for his threads, fantastic fabric finds are everywhere. When you find fabric with a great color or pattern, buy it—you'll find a use for it somewhere. For $3 a bolt, Brazilian tie-dye cotton in orange, yellow, and fuchsia inspired the funky vibe in this living room—even the painted toenail! Covering pillows with the bright fabric stretches a limited resource and makes the basic white slipcovers on the sofa and chair look even cleaner and crisper. *To see how easy it is to make such pillows, turn to page 142.*

White Plus a Color ▼

Doug's room illustrates a surefire trick for reviving a room: Start with one color and make it pop by teaming it with bright white. In this case, mustard yellow offers a rich backdrop for a crisp collection of elements transformed by a few coats of white paint. White paint not only makes the lackluster wood coffee table sparkle, it enhances the new framing above the fireplace, *opposite,* and elevates the room's cathedral ceiling to create a dramatic architectural focal point.

65

Stencil Fun ▲

Doug dressed up the walls with stencils inspired by flowery sarongs he purchased in Brazil for a mere $3 each. To create a stencil, Doug and one homeowner traced the outline of the fabric pattern and transferred it to stencil acetate. Look for stencil acetate at crafts and hobby stores and put a new blade in your crafts knife. The design of your handmade stencil can be inspired by almost anything: fabrics, wallpaper, photos, architectural elements, or your imagination. Whatever your inspiration, err on the side of simplicity. (After Doug began cutting the stencil, he decided to switch to a simpler design to meet the project deadline; he added a freehand dab of fuchsia paint to the center of his stenciled daisies.) One little footnote: The funky trio of painted canvases is a graphic rendering of Doug's bare foot. The homeowner confessed to a foot phobia, and this artwork—complete with fuchsia toenail—is the culmination of some good-natured teasing.

A Punch of Black ▲

White and bright is the dominant theme of Doug's Brazil-inspired room; a few dark touches, strategically placed throughout the space, provide the visual contrast needed to make the room interesting and to tame it with understated elegance. The dark wood table and chairs, *opposite* (which appear almost black) and the trio of black iron candlestands look smashing against the mustard wall. A director's chair with black canvas for the seat and back (see page 64) lends another notable dark touch in the conversation area.

Almost all furniture and accessories, such as frames and lamp bases, look more stylish and sophisticated donned in black. (Think how one little dress, fabricated from wonderful black fabric, makes a classic statement. Or how cool Zorro looks in all black.)

The gray window treatment fabric has similar dramatic power. Note how the fabric has two distinct, dark faces—one side is charcoal; the other silver. Alternating panels of the two-sided fabric creates a sophisticated striped effect for windows, slipcovers, and walls.

67

More Flower Power

Pick up lively, instant color on your way home from work.

Though Doug's stenciled flowers never need watering, a room-brightening bouquet of fresh flowers brings added life to the room. The orange glads pick up on the tones in the pillows and pull the color further into the room and up onto the mantel. If you want your investment to last longer, create an arrangement of quality silk flowers.

Ready-Made Slipcovers
For a dash of fast color, get ready-mades that measure up.

Here are three reasons to love slipcovers: (1) They make old furniture look like new; (2) they can introduce smashing new colors into a room to suit the season or your mood; (3) you can toss them in the washing machine whenever they're soiled or when you want to rinse away allergens.

It's no longer necessary to fuss with making your own slipcovers (unless you want to) or to pay a professional to sew custom covers for you. Attractive, ready-made, better-fitting slipcovers are now available in nearly unlimited colors, patterns, fabrics, and styles, through home stores and mail order catalogs and on the Internet. When ordering from catalogs or online, you'll most likely find information telling you how to measure furniture in order to select the correct size. If you're heading for the home store, plan on taking a few measurements with you to help you bring home the right ready-mades.

For sofas and armchairs, measure from the outside of one arm to the outside of the opposite arm. Some manufacturers may require that you take three measurements from your sofa or armchair, as shown in the illustrations (A, B, C). To choose a nicely fitted slipcover for an ottoman, measure the width, length, and height of the piece (D).

You'll even find ready-made slipcovers available for wing chairs (measure across the back from wing to wing), recliners (take these measurements: outside arm to outside arm, the back from floor to top, the width of the back, and the width of the footrest), and armless dining chairs (measure the length and width of the seat, as well as the back of the chair from the floor to the top).

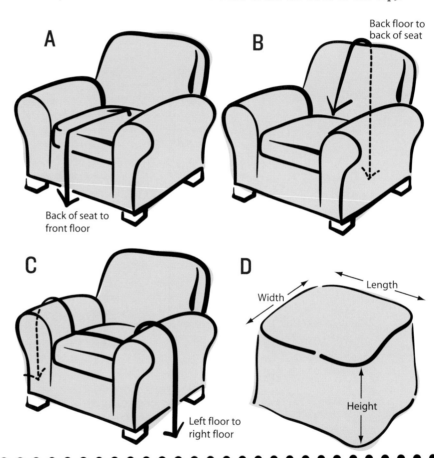

A — Back of seat to front floor

B — Back floor to back of seat

C — Left floor to right floor

D — Width, Length, Height

No More Arm Wrestling
A quick and easy fix for droopy arms on upholstered pieces

Shopping for ready-made slipcovers brings up the challenge of fitting sofa and chair arms. You might find it handy to take along a tracing that outlines the basic shape of the front of the arm. Then check the manufacturer's packaging to see if the slipcover suits your style of arm.

Take a cue from the *Trading Spaces* designers and overcome out-of-shape arms and uncomfortable cushions or backs by using thick layers of acrylic batting (available at crafts and fabric stores). Before applying the slipcover, wrap a layer or two (or more!) of acrylic batting around wimpy arms, backs, and cushions to plump them up and give them a sexier shape. If needed, spray adhesive can secure the batting in place. Stapling around the edges of the batting will also keep it in place, but don't try this on cushions or backs, or the staples could pop out and poke you!

68

Give 'em the Slip

Who knew slipcovers could be beautiful and versatile? The *Trading Spaces* designers, of course. Episode after episode, they transform has-beens into fab focal points.

Make colors pop. Complementary colors (such as the purple and pistachio green linens Hildi used on the dining room chairs in Alpharetta: Providence Oaks) pack a major visual punch. Simply sew pieces of two fabrics together; then fit the newly created large piece of fabric to each piece of furniture.

Create unity. In Austin: Wing Road, Hildi brought unity to a living room furniture set by slipcovering the seating in sleek silver fabric. To ensure a tight fit, pin the fabric on the furniture with the wrong side out, stitch the fabric together along the pinned lines, and turn right side out when re-covering.

Go for a tight fit. Slipcovers don't need to be shapeless. Laurie's store-bought red and black slipcovers for a living room in Miami: 168th/83rd look elegant and tailored. Tuck PVC piping or a thick dowel rod between the back of the furniture and the cushions on top of the slipcover fabric to help keep the fabric from coming untucked each time someone sits down.

Put ugly fabrics under wraps. Vern covered a hideous orange plaid thrift store couch in a Portland: Rosemont Avenue living room with a handmade black cotton twill slipcover. Twill is a great fabric choice for frequently used furniture because it is machine-washable.

Get a great look in less time. Rather than trying to spray-paint over several pieces with different upholstery (*à la* Hildi in Seattle: 56th Place), purchase ready-made slipcovers in the same color and give a room a unified look in less time.

Chapter 4: Warming Trend Like a crackling fire in a fireplace, the right color choices can help a room cast off the cold shoulder and make you feel cozy and instantly comfortable. Turn the page to experience warmth the *Trading Spaces* way.

70

WARMING TREND

Before

Though the vaulted ceilings were definitely an architectural bonus in this master bedroom, the green walls didn't give the homeowners the visual lift they were looking for. Doug came prepared to punch up the space with spectacular color.

72

Autumn Harvest

Doug makes a master bedroom glow with warmth.

COLOR LESSON: Bright, bold colors can be warm and soothing too.
BACKGROUND: In this Midwestern master suite, Doug starts with daringly deep orange and shows how mixing in soft contrasting hues and textural elements such as fabric can tone down the bold palette and make a space glow with warmth.

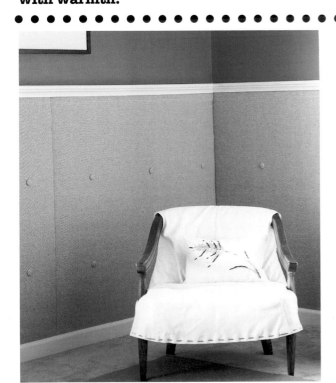

Orange Crush ◄

One deep color can seem overly powerful, but that doesn't mean you should avoid it in quiet, reflective spaces. Doug warmed the walls with an energizing swath of orange. Acting like a warm blanket, the deep hue turns up the temperature in visual terms and makes the room feel more inviting. The ceiling, a new chair rail, bedding, and slipcovers for a pair of armchairs infuse the room with enough white to make the orange as refreshing as a crisp fall day.

Soft-Touch Walls ◄

Rather than paint the walls all orange, Doug opted for 48-inch-tall wainscoting upholstered in muted gray heavy-weave cotton, which he purchased for $4.50 a yard or $100 total. To provide a sturdy surface for stapling on layers of batting and fabric, Amy Wynn removed the baseboards from the walls and attached 4×8-foot sheets of plywood. Fabric-covered buttons add a stylish dressmaker detail to the wainscoting.

73

Armoire in a Row ▶

When Doug asked Amy Wynn to build a substantial armoire to suit this large-volume room, she knew a single hefty piece might not fit up the stairs. By constructing the armoire in three side-by-side sections, she gave Doug a storage piece that's even larger than he had hoped for. White paint plays up the traditional-style paneled construction and pairs the piece with the chairs, which are slipcovered in white canvas.

Palette Aplenty ▶

Twin paintings of waving stalks of wheat, painted by Doug, gracefully repeat the orange and white palette and emphasize a fitting harvest theme for the room.

The four white pillowcases cost less than $35. Simple bands of orange ribbon take the pillowcases from plain to pretty with only a few stitches. One spool of ribbon cost a mere $1.89. "Fairly inexpensive for a high-end look," Doug says. Xs embroidered in orange give a plain white comforter a style boost.

Cedarwood shelves, mounted on fabric-covered braces on each side of the bed, offer surfaces for storage and display.

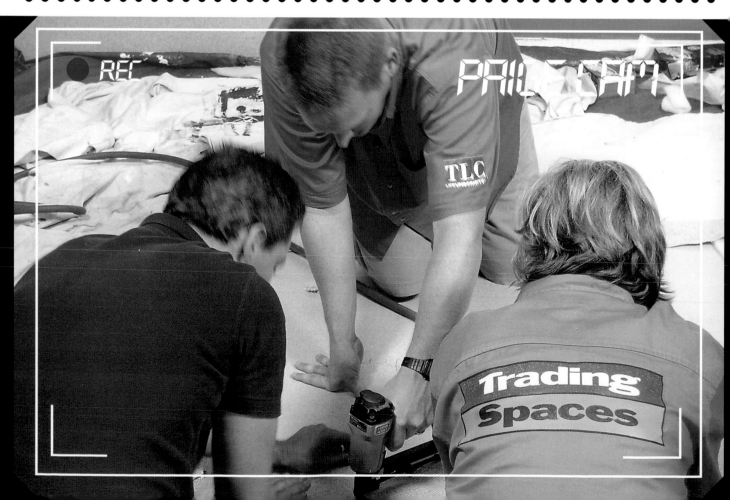

Bagging Bargain Fabrics

Low-cost fabric can introduce high-drama color.

Take a cue from the *Trading Spaces* designers and only rarely pay retail for fabrics to finish your room. Search through the sale tables at fabric stores or visit discount or factory-outlet fabric stores for the best prices. Also check garage and estate sales for bolts of leftovers at bargain prices.

Painters' drop cloths offer lots of yardage for a little bit of money, as do sheets. Both can convert into duvet covers, pillows, or window treatments.

Vintage fabrics are another option. If you're a savvy shopper, you may find chenille bedspreads starting at $15, solid-color linen or cotton tablecloths for $10 to $30, fruit tablecloths from the '40s for $8 to $15, and tea towels for $3 to $7. Think of these items as yardage instead of ready-to-use pieces.

Some basic fabrics also offer good value for your money. Consider canvas at $4 a yard, muslin as low as $1.50 a yard, mosquito netting at $4 a yard, cotton gauze at $3 a yard, and cotton broadcloth at $7 a yard. Netting and gauze offer lots of no-sew window options if you drape the fabric around curtain rods.

While you're bargain hunting, check out more expensive fabrics. If you find a stunning piece, purchase a small amount and use it as an accent in a room.

Soft-Touch Walls

Upholstered walls are a textural variation on classic wainscoting. Purchasing or renting a quality staple gun can help you complete this project quickly, securing batting and fabric directly to drywall or paneling with ease. Add finishing touches, such as covered buttons, fabric trims, or decorative wooden moldings for a grace note of refinement.

Remove any existing baseboard or other trim. Using a pencil and a carpenter's level, begin by marking a level line at the height where you want the upholstered section to end. (You can upholster a wall from floor to ceiling, if you wish.)

Use a staple gun with ¾-inch staples to secure the top edge of 12-ounce polyester batting to the wall (A). Pull the batting taut and abut batting sheets edge-to-edge with no gaps at the seams. Staple the bottom edge as well as the sides, smoothing the batting as you work.

Cut fabric, if necessary, to fit the wall. Staple the fabric to the wall (B), following the same method as for the batting.

Where lengths of fabric abut, cover the seam with decorative cording or ribbon glued into place with a glue gun.

To create a tufted look, mark locations where you want to place buttons. Use a carpenter's level for this step so that buttons remain in straight rows (C). At each mark, place two staples in an X. Use a glue gun to secure one covered button over each pair of staples (D).

Button Cover-Ups

To make your own covered buttons, start with a kit from a fabric or crafts store. You'll find a number of sizes, but the 1- to 2-inch sizes are often easier to cover and show up nicely on a wall or pillow. Using scraps of fabric, cut a circle ⅝ inch larger than the button form. Baste around the circle, using large stitches and leaving long tails (E). Fold the fabric over the base, tightly gathering the threads and securing them with a knot. Position the back button half on the fabric-covered half and press firmly to join.

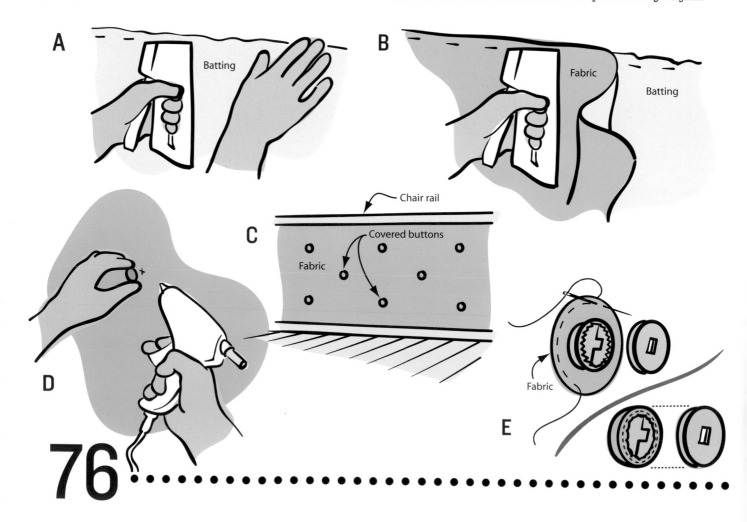

A Batting

B Fabric — Batting

C Chair rail — Covered buttons — Fabric

D

E Fabric

Creations on Canvas

Let that empty space of a blank canvas inspire you; fill it with your imagination. These ideas will spark your own fresh creations.

Get the gang together. Invite people over and put them to work with small canvases and a limited color palette. Because all the paintings have the same colors, they can be grouped attractively, even if their subject matter is wildly different. In California: Peralta Street, Doug and his homeowners painted canvases in the same palette to decorate dining room walls.

Ditch the paint. Canvas can hold more than paint. Display leaves, pieces of fabric, or art papers with decoupage medium or hot glue. In Austin: Wampton Way, Doug covered a large canvas with decoupaged newspaper spreads from that day's paper, thus decorating the room and commemorating the experience at the same time.

Set yourself free. Don't sweat it if you aren't the best artist on the block. Fill your blank canvas with free-form or taped-off abstract shapes until you're happy with the look. Laurie quickly created a striking abstract painting with only one color—black—in a living room in Wake Forest: Rodney Bay.

Spread it out. Spread a large image over several canvases and hang them all together. This creates a neat optical effect and can help break up a large expanse of wall. Laurie spread her concentric rectangle painting over two canvases in a living room in Houston: Sawdust Street.

No canvas? No problem! Be inventive and make your own if you don't have access to the real thing. A piece of wood, poster board, or the wall itself can do in a pinch. Frank spread joint compound over a piece of plywood and used that as his canvas in a living room in New Jersey: Perth Road.

Hollywood Glamour

COLOR LESSON: Warm up classic black and white.
BACKGROUND: This media room reflects the elegance of old Hollywood and features a cast of classic neutral colors and plush fabrics. Directed by Vern, this surefire hit could come to a (home) theater near you.

Trade Stuffy for Sophisticated ◀

Classic black and white can be sexy and sultry with the addition of warm taupe into the scheme. This loft living area offered Vern a chance to address the homeowners' request for "something fun." An animal print and plush black velvet fabrics ignited "a whole 1930s Hollywood glamour look," Vern says.

Custom-made sofas featuring black-painted bases and plump black-velvet-covered cushions step in as sophisticated replacements for the homeowners' old couches, which were given the ax. Picking up on the sofa design, a custom-made coffee table also features a black base and cushioned sections on top. Marble tiles in the center of the table provide a "resting spot" for beverages and knickknacks. Space under the table provides out-of-the-way but accessible storage.

For lighting that fits the vintage theater theme, a new "crystal chandelier" is actually a $2.50 light kit combined with a $39 shade originally intended for candles.

Film Stars ▼

With the velvet fabric in limited supply, Vern gains the most impact by using it thoughtfully, covering the sofa cushions and as the triangular highlights on the pillows. Not enough velvet was left over to cover the corner section of the sofa, so the base of that section serves as a practical occasional table.

On the tabletop, photos of Hollywood legends were photocopied onto vellum "so they're translucent," Vern says. Clear frames and votive backlighting create the illusion that the photos are clips right out of old movies.

On the walls, *opposite,* film stars take center stage—each framed in bold black and suspended from wires and eyehooks.

79

Before

By the time the homeowners finished decorating the rest of their house, they admit they had run out of ideas for this loft area. Now they're ready for some fun.

Darling, They're Diamonds ▲

You won't be counting karats with these diamonds, but you can count on comfort. Vern upholstered plywood squares with batting and taupe fabric—both stapled to the back of the squares. Industrial-strength hook-and-loop tape secures the "diamonds" to the wall but allows them to be removed if one becomes stained or the homeowners tire of the look. This wall treatment adds softness and style; it's also a practical design for a media room because the fabric and batting absorb sound. *For more nifty ideas for using hook-and-loop tape, turn to page 82.*

For more nifty ideas for using hook-and-loop tape, turn to page 82.

Starring Attraction ▶

An alcove is a perfect spot for setting a stage. Shelves, more framed film stars on vellum, and taupe curtain panels edged in velvet transform the ordinary niche into a knockout entertainment center.

Neutral Territory

Switzerland isn't the only place that can enjoy being neutral.

New hues—many with a playful undertone—are joining the neutral ranks.

Uncomplicated, beautiful, simple, honest, pure, and dressy—a neutral color scheme can be all this and more. Shades of white, tan or beige, and gray and black make up the foundation of the hues traditionally defined as neutral. (Many designers are now also welcoming colors such as green into the neutral fold.) When you combine the three basic neutrals, keep these suggestions in mind:

Vary the shades. Even white comes in a bundle of shades. Whether you mix three neutral colors (black, white, and tan, for example) or decide on a one-color scheme, spice up the look by including more than one shade of your chosen color. Off-white, cream, and ivory, for example, are three shades of white that will create an instantly elegant decor.

Return to black and white. The high-contrast pairing of black and white just oozes drama but also can make a room feel serene and soothing. Give this classic two-color combo a little punch with texture and the bold, graphic shapes of artwork, sculpture, and curvaceous furniture.

Go easy on the accents. If you decide on a neutral theme, be careful not to add too much accent color. Keep colored accessories simple and few, or you may detract from your overall scheme.

> **One way to make a room look expensive when you don't have a lot of money,"** Vern says, **"is to use your nice fabric sparingly.**

Hook-and-Loop Tape Tricks

Try some decorating magic of your own.

What goes up must come down. Hook-and-loop tape allows both installation and removal to be done in record-setting time.

The hooklike shape of cockleburs and their natural stick-to-itiveness inspired the invention of hook-and-loop tape—a product that's right up there with two other decorating must-haves: glue guns and fusible webbing. You'll find hook-and-loop tape—one popular brand is Velcro—in many permutations, including some with adhesive backs on one or both strips or extra-wide superstrength strips for hanging heavier objects. After you get used to having hook-and-loop tape around the house, you'll discover a wide variety of uses. Here's a brief sampler of ideas:

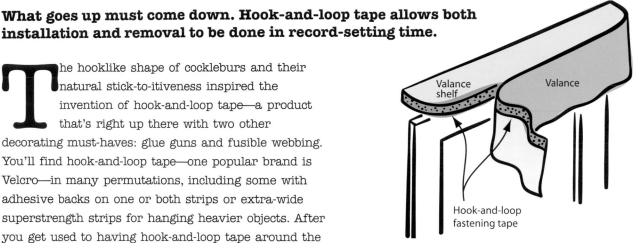

Valance shelf

Valance

Hook-and-loop fastening tape

Window Topper. Stitch one half of the hook-and-loop strip to the back of a window treatment and affix the adhesive backing on the opposing strip to the window casing or an extended cornice. To hang, press the strips together.

Sink Sense. Dress up a pedestal or wall-hung sink with a fabric skirt, using hook-and-loop tape along the top edge of the fabric and around the outside top edge of the sink. The skirt looks great and creates storage below the sink.

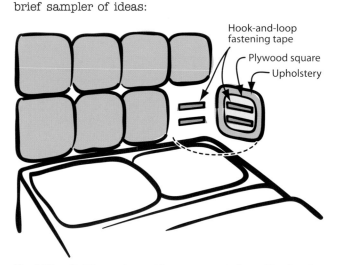

Hook-and-loop fastening tape

Plywood square

Upholstery

Bed Head. Use extra-wide commercial-quality hook-and-loop tape to hang artwork at the head of the bed. Or, as Vern often does, stick upholstered squares to the wall as a headboard or full-wall treatment.

Hook-and-loop fastening tape

Skirt

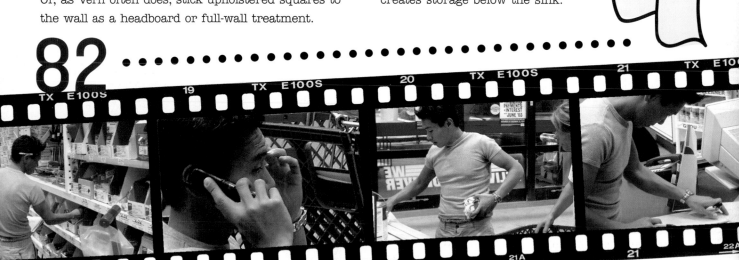

Tabletop Style

Vern used a collection of old photos to form a focal point on the sofa table. Consider these other attention-grabbing tabletop ideas for any room of your home.

Pile it on. Even the most mundane decorative items can become extraordinary when displayed together in a group. When selecting items, choose one specific aspect to focus on—such as color, shape, or function—and the grouping will become a cohesive whole. In Seattle: l37th Street, Doug used this technique with taper candleholders on a living room coffee table.

Twist the traditional. Fresh flowers are a classic decorative choice, but consider experimenting with unconventional displays. Float a single bloom in a bowl of water or scatter petals across a tabletop. Vern displayed a bouquet of white flowers in a vase filled with fruit in a Portland: Rosemont Avenue living room.

Hit the produce aisle. Bowls of fresh fruit are a must in the kitchen for fast and easy snacking, but scattering them around the house lends an organic look and bright color to any room. In Portland: Rosemont Avenue, Laurie fills two large glass containers with green apples to decorate a living room mantel.

Scatter a little here and there. Spread small piles of shells, pebbles, beads, or buttons around other decorative items, such as candles or frames, to create a loose, free-flowing look. Doug spread beans around two blue gazing balls in his "Time Flies" kitchen in Austin: Wycliff.

Break out the crafts supplies. Instead of grouping items together, combine them into something different. Connect antique spools with twine or cover different plastic foam shapes with silk flowers to create tabletop sculptures. In a living room in Texas: Sutton Court, Frank decorated a mantel with cactus made from vegetables and flower blooms.

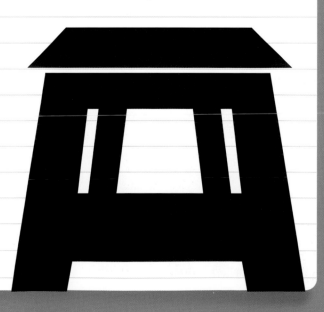

Geometry Class

COLOR LESSON: Make a big room more livable with earth tones.
BACKGROUND: This master bedroom is so big that the homeowners' sons played football in it. With warm colors and geometric details, Doug transforms the room into two beautiful, intimate spaces.

Divide and Conquer ◀

Color and construction combined to make this space an intimate adult retreat. First, Doug built an H-shape partial wall unit that divides the oversize master bedroom into two practical spaces. The wall leaves plenty of walking room on each side; stopping short of the ceiling makes the structure less imposing. This end of the room offers a sitting area. Orange paint the color of bittersweet covers the MDF-constructed wall and makes the sitting area seem cozy and warm. Buttercream yellow on the surrounding walls helps keep the room from feeling too dark. Pillows in bittersweet, featuring black velvet appliquéd squares, bring color and a playful sense of motion to the oyster-tone sofa.

Anchors Aweigh ◀

To define and anchor the seating area, Doug made a small area rug for about $24 by backing a piece of rust-red wool with a canvas drop cloth. Spray-mount adhesive holds the pieces together. Serving as a landing spot for books and beverages, this coffee table constructed by Ty features wood slats formed into concentric rectangles atop wooden bracket-style legs. A black vase adds a dash of funk.

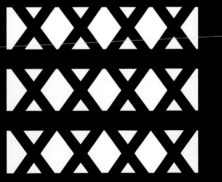

85

Testing, Testing...1-2-3...

Test a little paint before you buy a lot.

To test a paint color before committing to an entire gallon or more, buy a quart or a test-size sample and paint a small area. Live with it for several days. Observe how the color changes under different light. For a more accurate portrayal, brush the color onto a large sheet of poster board and place the giant paint chip in different parts of the room, especially near different pieces of furniture.

Testing with real paint is important because color usually appears somewhat "bigger than life" after it's actually on the wall. Color offers more impact than you might expect, especially when you brush it onto all four walls.

Squarely Stylish ◀

Starting with wool lining in an earthy rust tone, Doug used squares of buttercream yellow and black velvet to dress up the fabric and turn it into an artistic comforter and pillowcases. The rich bittersweet wall color continues from the opposite side of the wall, so lamps were added to prevent the space from appearing too dark.

Remember that paint color often dries darker on the wall than it appears in the can—or even on the paint card. Before painting the entire room, paint a test spot, let dry, and see how you like it.

87

Fabric Appliqués

Easily embellish fabric by layering on more fabric. And you don't even have to know how to sew!

Appliqués are ideal for adding style to purchased pillows as well as unadorned comforters, sheets, table linens, and window treatments. Here's how easy appliqués are to do—even if you're not big on sewing: Start with a panel of fabric. (If you have scraps lying around, this is a great way to use them.) Cut the panel into any shape you like, adding ½ inch all around for seam allowances. Turn under the excess and press with an iron. Pin in place on the fabric, and using matching thread, whipstitch as shown, all the way around the appliqué. For a more dramatic look, use a contrasting thread color or use yarn or embroidery floss instead of thread.

Embellish appliqués with buttons, beadwork, ribbons, and iron-on transfers for even more interest and fun.

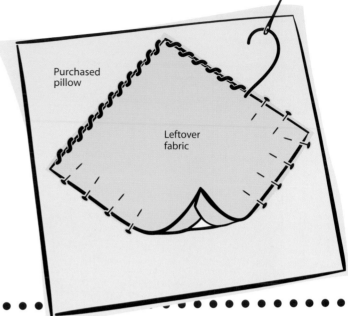

Purchased pillow

Leftover fabric

"When you take something very plain," Doug says, "and dress it up in a simple way with a little bit of pattern, it goes a long way.

Geometric Designs

What better way to shape up a room than with shapes? These creative looks all have roots in simple geometric forms.

Create a focal point. Add a geometric pattern to a pillow, an accessory, or an art piece. Even a small touch of geometry can make a big statement and draw the eye. Laurie created a lovely focal point by painting a geometric faux-inlay tabletop in a living room in Chicago: Edward Road.

Create one large geometric statement. Rather than add a few geometric details, be bold and make the whole room geometric. That's how Hildi created her design for a living room in California: Peralta Street. She divided everything in the room into quadrants—from the paint colors to draperies to upholstery.

Create an interlocking design. Use a stamp or stencil of a simple shape and repeat or overlap it. This technique adds a fun, graphic touch to furniture, draperies, or even rugs. In a living room in Los Angeles: Willoughby Avenue, Doug covered all the walls, including the doors, with a large red and white pattern of modified squares.

Create contrast with geometry. The eye can become bored looking at the same shape over and over. Add visual interest by throwing in an unexpected shape, like a round candlestick in an arrangement of rectangular ones. In an Egyptian-theme bedroom in Indianapolis: Halleck Way, Kia added a pyramid-shape pillow to a bed full of square pillows.

Create a three-dimensional look. Take your geometric design to the next level. Give flat two-dimensional shapes some depth. Gen dabbled in the next dimension by creating a wall of squares that jutted out at different depths into a living room in Oregon: Alyssum Avenue.

EXOTIC ADVENTURES

Chapter 5: Exotic Adventures Feel an urge to pack your bags and trek to new and unusual places? Looking for some international intrigue? This chapter shows you how to combine colors and elements associated with faraway lands and take an exotic adventure— right under your own roof.

91

Saying they are "cautiously open-minded" about the new design for their bedroom, the homeowners could not have guessed the "swinging" solution that Kia dreamed up.

Before

Unwind in India

Kia mingles images and elements from India with dynamic colors.

COLOR LESSON: Pick complementary colors for energy.
BACKGROUND: With the goal of "sensuality meets meditative," Kia deftly mixed Indian-influenced elements with an unexpected orange and blue color combo, and added a hanging bed as a fab focal point.

Magic Carpet Ride ◄

Complementary colors—like the blue and orange hues used in this bedroom—excite and energize with an almost exotic air. Taking a cue from an intricate wallpaper border, Kia clicked the color down several shades to arrive at a rich orange hue for the paint. Cobalt blue trim provides an enticing contrast. Using the orange paint and the wide wallpaper border on the coved portion of the ceiling coaxes the eye to look upward and appreciate the architecture. Off-white on the ceiling and some of the walls keeps intense colors from overpowering.

With visions of a flying carpet, Kia suspended the bed from heavy-duty chains (after beefing up the ceiling with additional lumber). Orange paint on the frame, a cobalt blue bedspread, and orange bolsters carry the color theme to the center of the room.

Pallet-able Pleasure ▼

Kia nabbed a freebie when she found a large wooden pallet in someone's trash. Sawed into sections, a portion of the pallet dresses up in cobalt blue and stands slightly higher on short legs to serve as an "altar" for displaying treasures; the lower bench provides a place to kneel. A length of silk on the tabletop and a trio of ceramic tiles on the bench feature India-inspired motifs in red and orange colors that work with the room.

Soothing Silks ▼

Silk always seems to say "India," and Kia generously used the fabric, as well as some silk look-alikes, to play up the exotic theme. This mustard-color silk pillow features a pattern that lends textural interest to the bed.

93

Salvage Savvy ▶

The pallet reappears in this bedroom sitting area: Two portions of it pair up as display shelves on vibrant orange walls. The space is made more mysterious and secluded by the addition of some ancient-looking columns with a weathered-blue stain finish. Deep blue sheer fabric heightens the sense of intrigue.

The Eighth Wonder ▲

As a clever cover-up for ordinary shelves, Ty built a
plywood surround with a cutout reminiscent of Indian
architecture. A cardboard template made it easy to
transfer the shape of the cutout to the plywood. Orange
paint makes the surround stand out from the off-white
wall behind the shelves.

More Salvage Style ▲

Salvage brings ancient yet chic style to the window.
The valance is actually a stairway baluster turned on
its side and attached to the window frame with screws.
Orange sheer fabric lends a soft touch.

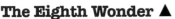 **95**

COLORING LESSONS

Using Contrasting Colors
Opposites really do attract! Try them at home.

Hankering to add some serious pizzazz to a
room? Consider contrasting—or in Color Wheel-
ese (see page 27), *complementary*—hues. Located on
opposite sides of the color wheel, complementary colors
appear more vivid when placed side by side. To experience
this effect, glance at Kia's Indian-inspired bedroom and see
how the orange appears more orange and the blue, bluer;
these are contrasting hues—they pop when paired.

The other contrasting color schemes are red with green
and purple with yellow. To create variety with any of these
complementary palettes, simply include various intensities of
each color within the room. Because complementary color
schemes always include one warm and one cool color, they
naturally balance one another.

If you're feeling a little color-shy, but you like the idea of

adding drama with contrasting color, start at a more
comfortable level. Begin with neutral walls and furniture and
add colorful accents and accessories that capture your
fancy. After you live with the look for a while and you decide
you love it, kick up the color quotient with either more
accessories or some upholstered or painted furnishings.
Consider painting the walls and trim in your complementary
palette, as Kia did here. If this approach is out of your
comfort zone, paint trim the deepest shade on the paint chip
and paint walls the palest tint on the opposing chip. To make
the trim stand out even more, choose a semigloss sheen;
select a satin or flat sheen for the walls.

Even if related, or analogous, hues are more your style, it's
often best to toss in a dollop of contrasting color to energize
the room and make the setting more striking.

Hanging Borders

It's only a thin strip of decorative paper, but a border offers big style for a few bucks.

If you need a quick flash of style, consider adding wall border to a space. Look for prepasted borders, and this project goes faster than you might expect.

1 Prepare it. Wipe down the walls you plan to paper. If you're hanging border on recently painted walls, allow the paint to dry completely.

2 Mark it. Stand in the room and pick a corner that isn't noticeable when entering—that's where you should start the border. If you're planning a chair rail-height border, mark the top edge using a pencil and a level (A).

3 Book it. In order to activate the paste on the back of the paper, you need to perform a step called "booking." This means folding the border so the water can penetrate the adhesive. Fill a tray with water and add the rolled length of border. Let sit for a minute or so (follow the manufacturer's directions). Pull the

border out of the water, holding on to one short edge of the strip and allowing it to unroll as you remove it from the tray. Now fold the strip back and forth accordion-style as shown (B) if the manufacturer suggests this type of fold. Be careful not to flatten the folds.

4 Hang it. Find a second pair of hands to help hang your border. One person can hold the border while the other unfolds the strip, positions it, and smoothes it with a wallpaper brush (C).

5 Seam it. If you must create a seam in the middle of a wall, overlap the two strips. Cut through the two thicknesses using a utility knife and a straightedge (D); peel away the cut pieces and press the seam into place.

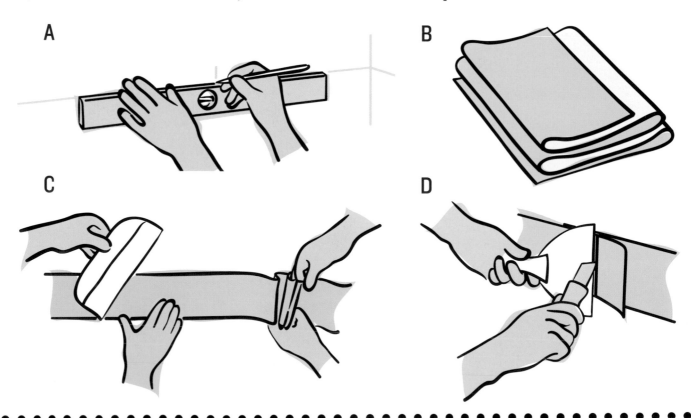

A

B

C

D

ORANGE has always been a color for adventurous spirits. Kia's bedroom shows that orange has two sides: Yes, orange can be fun—even a little mischievous—but its natural warmth also makes orange a good choice for wrapping a space in peace and tranquillity.

Create a getaway in your home by bringing in colors, textures, and materials from faraway places.

Choose a bold theme. Instead of starting your redecorating with a color choice, give your room an unusual, exotic theme. Spend time daydreaming and look to travel magazines or your own vacation photos for inspiration. Vern designed a resort hotel look in a bedroom in California: Corte Rosa, creating a rich romantic atmosphere.

Choose bold—everything! Pull together exotic paint colors, fabrics, and furniture to put your room over the top. The bolder the better! Doug painted zebra stripes on all the walls, built primitive furniture, and even hung stuffed monkeys from the ceiling in his "Jungle Boogie" fantasy bedroom in Pennsylvania: Gorski Lane.

Choose bold colors. Set an exotic mood by painting with a lush palette. Translate the beautiful blue of the Caribbean Sea or the rich orange of a sunset into paint colors. In Indianapolis: Halleck Way, Kia painted an Egyptian-theme bedroom with colors she named "Tut Wine" and "Pharaoh Gold."

Choose bold furniture. Find furniture that could be in a resort hotel. You don't have to buy all new pieces—look at your existing furniture with new eyes. A little paint or new hardware may be all an old dresser needs to fit in with your new theme. In Missouri: Sunburst Drive, Gen pulled dark-stained pieces from other rooms to give an Argentine feel to a bedroom.

Choose bold fabrics. Plush upholstery and gauzy canopies lend a far-off feel to any room. Get inspiration by wandering the aisles of your local fabric store to see what gets you thinking of distant lands. Gen draped a teenager's bed with layers of sheer gold fabric in an Indian-theme bedroom in Cincinnati: Sturbridge Road—with spectacular results.

Arabian Nights Revisited

COLOR LESSON: Accent with gold and silver for a regal flair.
BACKGROUND: When Gen traveled to Arizona to redo this living area for two young college-age women, she found a large space with unattractive surfaces. Red, gold, and yards of featherlight muslin fabric help shape an exotic atmosphere that appears fresh from the pages of a fairy tale.

Visions of Opulence ◀

Metallic tones—like the golden throw pillows and shimmering ceiling draperies in this room—add richness to any space. The ceiling in this living area may appear peaked, but that's an illusion created by the gossomerlike fabric. The centers of long fabric panels are attached to the ceiling with a long painted board. The panels swag downward to the wall, where another wood strip keeps them in position. The fabric finally cascades down brightly colored walls, gathered here and there by gold tiebacks. Deep red walls and a wide gold-leaf stripe set the stage for a pair of sofas featuring wood bases and cushions covered in blue polka-dot silk. Plump gold bolsters, a black-painted coffee table (made extra low by cutting the legs shorter), and floor pillows complete the look.

Lights Fantastic ◀

Two blue and silver silk shades with dangling crystal accents lend a luxurious look to the lighting overhead.

Chevreul's Laws

These tips may be a blast from the past, but hey, they work!

COLORING LESSONS

In the 19th century, a chemist by the name of **Michel Chevreul** noticed that colors had a definite effect on one another when positioned as neighbors. These effects, known as Chevreul's Laws, may be helpful as you choose colors for your rooms. Here are some nifty nuggets of color science that Chevreul discovered:

✳ Placed on a dark background, light colors stand out.
✳ White or light colors make all colors more noticeable.
✳ Dark colors against dark colors don't stand out, but contrast dark colors on a light background, and you can't miss 'em.
✳ Light colors against light colors don't stand out either, but put the same light color on a dark background, and suddenly, the light color appears lighter.

✳ Place two colors next to each other, and they tint one another with their own complement. Huh? Stated another way: Place a pair of complementary colors together and they appear to intensify in value.
✳ Outline colors in black, and the color intensifies. (That's why black accents look so cool in a room.)
✳ Outline dark colors in a thin white or light-color border, and the dark color intensifies. (White makes colors pop, remember?)

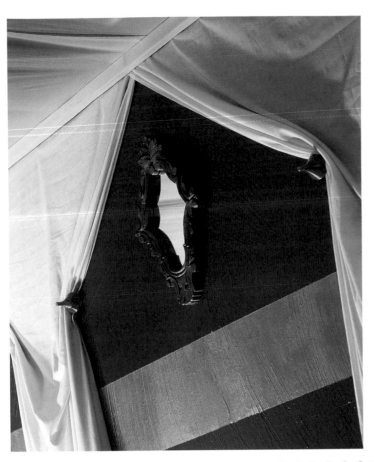

Reflections of Grandeur ◄

A diamond-shape mirror with an ornate gold frame seems made for this spot between fabric panels. To keep the panels pulled back, Gen found these unusual knobs, which are screwed into the stucco.

Mastering a Gallery ◄

One long wall inspired this gallerylike decorating strategy. Favorite photos taken during the shooting of the episode are framed in fours and elegantly spaced with candle sconces—directly above the gold leaf stripe. Serving as a display or buffet ledge, an unusual table built by Ty features thin bands of wood holding white PVC caps at the centers.

In a small space, always use furniture that can serve two purposes. The console, for example, pulls away from the wall to become a beverage bar during parties. The broad sofas are comfortable for overnight guests.

If flowers aren't in this week's budget, consider a shapely container filled above the brim with an assortment of colorful fruits. It's an easy centerpiece—edible too!

Arranging Flowers

Flowers are a fast, flexible, and fun way to inject color into a space. To create your own stunning (and stress-free!) flower arrangements, follow these guidelines:

✱ Floral shops aren't the only places where flowers are available. Florists and online resources may offer many varieties, but local farmer's markets, roadside ditches, and, of course, your own garden boast homegrown specials.

✱ Ordinary vases are OK, but why not use a container that's a little unexpected, such as a vintage teapot, an old boot, or a woven basket. (Simply line nonwaterproof items with a glass or plastic container.)

✱ Display single specimens—a beautiful rose bud or a delicate iris—in a bud vase. Use soda bottles, test tubes, or champagne flutes as a stand-in for a traditional bud vase.

✱ Remove stems and leaves and float lush rose or mum blossoms in open containers like cut-glass bowls, terra-cotta planters, or plastic partyware.

✱ Provide your flowers with adequate moisture by anchoring them in florist's foam or a full vase of water.

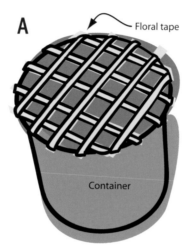

A — Floral tape

Container

B

When using a vase or container without a florist's frog or foam, encourage stems to stay put by crisscrossing the top of the container with florist's tape (A). Decorative marbles or pebbles can also be used to help flowers stand straight.

✱ Depending on the look you want, choose several or only a few of one kind of flowers for dramatic impact; or use armloads of different colors and varieties. Consider a monochromatic scheme of all blues, all whites, or whatever strikes your fancy.

✱ For an overflowing, casual look, position flowers, leaves, or vines to spill over the lip of the container to meet the tabletop (B). As you add stems, point flowers so they face outward, up, and down, working from the center of the container to the rim. Have filler material on hand, such as lacy ferns, petite flowers, or other greenery.

Mix up your color palette with flowers. Flowers transcend the rules of color—nearly every hue and all varieties fit in a room because they're a natural element. For visual impact, select flowers in one color and choose a variety of shades,

such as purples to lavenders.

Things Are Looking Up

Ceilings are rarely overlooked by the *Trading Spaces* designers so give your ceilings a special touch too.

Add the illusion of height. To make a low ceiling look higher, paint it the same color as the walls. The eye blends the wall into the ceiling and has trouble discerning a break between the two. Vern raised a ceiling with this technique in a red living room in Philadelphia: Jeannes Street.

Make it a focal point. Think of your ceiling as a large blank canvas. Stencil a pattern, freehand a colorful design, or use your favorite faux-painting technique to add visual interest. In Oregon: Alsea Court, Frank painted a serape-inspired design on a kitchen ceiling.

Go easy on your pocketbook. Crown molding adds a finished look to any room, but it can be expensive and time-consuming to install. Instead, tape off a few inches at the top of each wall and bring the ceiling paint down to meet the tape. When the tape is removed, you'll have a look similar to Gen's Argentine bedroom in Missouri: Sunburst Drive.

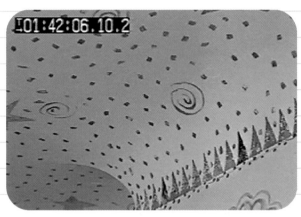

Highlight the details. Got angles, curves, or insets? Show them off! Use paint colors or patterns to accentuate any interesting architectural features. In Santa Clara: Lafayette Street, Frank used sponges to create multicolor stars and triangles that emphasized the curved design of the ceiling in a sorority chapter room.

Take it down a notch. Cathedral ceilings can be an asset in a grand entryway but can become a liability when you're trying to create an intimate mood. Bring things down to earth by painting the ceiling a darker color than the walls. Doug used this trick to disguise a high ceiling in a bedroom in San Diego: Dusty Trail.

ELEGANT ATTITUDE

Chapter 6: Elegant Attitude Just as the Eiffel Tower, ancient architecture, and classic films will never go out of style, elegant, timeless colors and the refined elements that go with them will be as lovely to look at a few years from now as they are today.

105

Tradition with a Twist

Laurie tweaks a timeless color palette.

COLOR LESSON: Perk up classic color combos for new looks.

BACKGROUND: Back on her home turf in Jackson, Mississippi, Laurie updates the classic color combination of tan and blue to camel and aqua in this master bedroom. An elegant look emerges as she unites the dynamic duo with traditional and contemporary elements.

Timeless Style for Y'all ◄

Tan and blue have long been a prized color pairing. So when Laurie found a brighter, more contemporary interpretation in a camel and aqua traditional plaid fabric, she knew it could serve as a unifier for classic and modern styles. While the plaid dresses up a bench cushion, French-style tapestrylike bedding in the same color duo introduces pattern variety. "I found the bedding at a salvage center," Laurie says. "I looked all over it for a flaw, but it is gorgeous."

To make the cool fabric colors "pop," Laurie opted for the camel color on the walls. Drawing attention to the grand proportions of the room and the 10-foot-high ceiling is a custom-made grid-style headboard. Aqua blue fabric, tucked behind the grid frame, pulls the color upward toward the ceiling. Another solid blue fabric serves as a bedskirt.

A new pair of bookshelves gives renewed importance to the fireplace; the coat of brown paint mimics mahogany for a rich look.

High Style ◄

Like the headboard, floor-to-ceiling aqua drapery panels lend color and softness and lure the eye upward. Wooden rings, stitched to the pleats, keep the look casual and relaxed.

Before

The homeowners want the fireplace to be the focal point in their master bedroom. One says the ceiling fan can go; the other says no. Guess who wins?

Reflections of Elegance ▲

Because purchasing a mirror large enough to fill the space above the fireplace mantel would have "cost a fortune," Laurie says, she cleverly substituted affordable mirror tiles. Construction adhesive secures the tiles on plywood backing, and screws keep the frame in place. Hammered-gold spray paint gives the wood frame an elegant finish.

Spray-Painting Tips

Whether you use spray paint to renew an old chandelier, dress up a wood frame, or renew an antique wicker chair. Here's how to get great results on all kinds of surfaces.

Prepare. Get the surface ready to receive the paint. For wood, glass, or plastic, use fine-grain sandpaper for a smooth start. Wipe up debris with a tack cloth. On metal objects, use sandpaper or a wire brush to minimize rust. Rub the surface with a degreaser to get rid of oil. For all these surfaces, apply a coat of primer and let dry.

Pick a day. You'll achieve the best finish if you work in low humidity. Work outdoors, when possible, but don't work in the direct sun or in high humidity. If you must work inside, arrange for adequate ventilation and run a fan.

Patience! Use drop cloths or several layers of newspaper to protect the area around the object you plan to spray-paint, and shake the can as long as the manufacturer suggests. To avoid drips and runs, apply two or three thin coats rather than one thick, gloppy coat. Point the can off the edge of the object (not directly on it), depress the spray button, and "glide" the can back and forth. With each pass, continue spraying off the edge of the object and release the spray button at the end of the pass. Repeat the procedure, slightly overlapping each pass, until the surface is lightly coated. Follow the manufacturer's directions for drying time between coats.

Classic Pairs

Like Bogey and Bacall, some pairs of colors seem to belong together. Many of them communicate a particular style. Consider these classics:

Blue and White	Country and French country kitchens could hardly get along without this refreshing twosome. Yet the look of these colors is so clean, they work well in contemporary settings too.
Blue and Tan	This peaceful pairing works anywhere you want to create an airy and relaxing atmosphere. Think sky and sand, as in Laurie's master bedroom, or tweak the shades to match your vision.
Black and White	You know those little hexagonal ceramic tiles so ubiquitous in bathrooms of the '20s and '30s? Black and white has always been a prized combination throughout the house, but the bathroom seems to be a favorite—most likely for the cleanliness that white evokes and the inherent elegance of black.
Red and Green	One of the more recent permutations of this color duet is forest green and burgundy—still favored by many for dressing a masculine study, for example. But you might also consider bottle green and berry red to brighten a kitchen or even a family room.
??? and ???	Of course, dozens of exciting color combos are possible. Use the color wheel information on page 21 to get your creative juices flowing, and have fun!

Creative Camouflage ▲

At first glance, this night table blends perfectly with the existing mahogany bedroom furniture (see a slice of the night table on the right side of the bed, page 106). This contemporary-style stand was custom-built for the makeover; however, it's wearing a budget-savvy disguise of brown paint. The camel background makes even this understated piece pop.

Glowing Reviews ▲

Somewhere out there, there are still bargains to be had, and Laurie proves it with this gorgeous chandelier that she purchased at a flea market for only $35. To dress it up, she lightly scuffed the original finish with sandpaper, primed the surface, and then transformed it with hammered-gold spray paint.

Beauty and the Bench ▶

A darkly stained rattan bench topped with a cushioned seat covered in one of the rooms coordinating fabrics acts like a bookend, finishing off the end of the bed. If you have the space available, almost any bedroom can benefit from the addition of a small bench. At the foot of the bed, a bench serves as a handy spot to sit down and put your shoes on. Benches with a boxlike construction can provide several cubic feet of additional storage space for blankets and linens. Plus, a bench that you upholster yourself provides yet another opportunity for bringing custom color and pattern into the boudoir.

Dress Up a Bench
Large or small, a bench offers comfort and color.

Can't find the right size and shape of bench for your space? Go custom and build a one-of-kind creation from scratch by following these ever-so-simple steps:

1 **Cut a piece of ½-inch plywood** to the desired size and shape. Screw on purchased turned legs—you'll find a huge selection at home centers—or make your own if you own a power lathe.

2 **Top the plywood** with one or more layers of foam. Check automotive interior suppliers and upholstery shops for the really comfy thick stuff. To ensure that the foam stays put, spray the plywood with upholstery adhesive and press the foam in place.

3 **To soften the corners,** stretch a layer or two of batting over the foam and over the edges of the plywood. Staple around the plywood edge to secure; trim off excess.

Fabric

Batting

Foam

Plywood

Fringe

4 **For a tufted bench,** mark where you want to place buttons. Thread a 4-inch

screw through a large washer, position the screw at a mark, and screw through the foam and into the plywood, creating a dimple for a button. Cover a button with scrap fabric (see page 76 for covered button how-to), and hot-glue a button over each washer.

5 **Lay fabric over the batting,** neatly folding ends around corners. Staple around edges or to the plywood bottom, whichever achieves the best look for the piece you're working on. Staple the ends in place first; then secure the sides.

6 **Use a hot-glue gun** to cover visible staples with fringe or cording.

110

Simply Elegant Ideas

You'll be surprised by the array of simple elements you can use to bring instant elegance into your rooms. Take a cue from these dashes of *Trading Spaces* class.

Shimmery elegance. Add refinement to your room by incorporating small bits of metallics. Silver or gold picture frames, candlesticks, or drapery finials are all ways of adding elegance to a design. Hildi added light-catching shimmer to a dining room in Austin: Wycliff by covering the ceiling with red and gold paper squares.

Effortless elegance. Lush fabrics or posh furnishings aren't really necessary. Simplicity is inherently elegant and easy to achieve. Look for the most straightforward way to get the look you want. In Maple Glen: Fiedler Road, Laurie appliquéd bamboo place mats to the front of white pillow shams, with stylish results.

Graceful elegance. Use small, dainty items throughout a room to create a light, charming look. Crystal, blown glass, or prisms work well and catch the light, ultimately brightening the room. Vern embellished a canopy with 100 suspended icicle-shape crystals in a bedroom in Maryland: Fairway Court.

Custom elegance. Although monograms have always been a stylish classic, personalization is back in a big way. Take your linens to a local tailor to be embroidered with your initials or do it yourself. If you can't sew, watch Hildi in Oregon: Alyssum Avenue. She used fabric paint to create a large monogram on a white bedspread in a romantic bedroom.

Repurposed elegance. Find a way to make everything old new again by adding antiqued embellishments to existing furnishings. Many antiques shops carry architectural salvage, such as filigreed vent covers, rescued stained-glass windows, and ornate doorknobs. Edward transformed glass shutters into bookshelf doors in a bedroom in Long Island: Dover Court.

Before

Stately style and old recliners don't mesh, so the recliners had to go. But what to do with all those windows?

Urban Renewal

We will redecorate by relocating!

COLOR LESSON: Vary one tone for refinement.
BACKGROUND: Kia gives an Austin, Texas, couple comfort and refinement with an all-encompassing cocoa color scheme. Touches of crisp white and a luxurious window treatment update a handsome traditional look.

Crazy for Cocoa ◄

In the world of monochromatic color schemes, "same" does not have to be "boring." Kia brought in a bevy of monochromatic fabrics—$500 worth, in fact—to wrap this room in warmth and elegance. With limited funds left for the rest of the room, an existing sofa stays put; luckily it pairs with the cocoa color to create a low-key, high-style look where cocoa is king.

Sheer Delights ▼

Tone-on-tone patterned swags—with ultragenerous gathers—create a rich and luscious layered effect when paired with lacy cocoa-color panels topped with wide bands of material that match the swags. The delicate lower fabric introduces an ornate element and allows sunlight to filter through and cast delicate patterns on the floor.

Relocate to Redecorate ▼

Knowing she would have to be careful with the remaining budget, Kia's motto became "redecorating by relocating." Because the makeover was consistent with the homeowners' love of warm color and elegance, existing accessories and furnishings, such as this lamp and occasional table, effortlessly melded into the new space.

113

BROWNS of all kinds appear in nature, so no wonder brown easily communicates strength and endurance. Use brown to create warmth in a room and to inspire a sense of permanence and graciousness.

Seating in a Snap ▲

Ready-to-assemble furniture, such as this daybed/settee, offers affordability and good looks. Painting the graceful iron frame gold and adding a cushion covered in a cocoa stripe fabric provides additional style and extra seating for little money. Pillows with some subtle punches of red increase comfort and color in the room.

Focus on the Fireplace ◄

While velvety cocoa paint topped with subtle gold glaze dresses up the fireplace wall, crisp white-painted molding added above the mantel makes the hearth a grand focal point. A gilt-frame mirror reflects the beautiful window treatments on the opposite wall. The existing black marble tiles pair nicely with the earthy tones.

Good Bones ▲

The room already featured some pleasing architecture, including an abundance of windows and this beautiful woodwork on the fireplace mantel. The clean white color sets off the cocoa tones on the surrounding walls, and the subtle shadows are all that's needed to make the moldings and flutes stand out.

COLORING LESSONS
Monochromatic Schemes

Decorating with essentially one color isn't boring at all, and it doesn't have to be neutral either. Choose tone-on-tone blues, greens, lavenders, yellows, reds—such as the bedroom designed by Vern, *right*—the choices are unlimited. The secret to successfully using a monochromatic scheme is to introduce a variety of shades selected from one color family. The paint color cards at home centers and paint stores make the selection process virtually mistake-proof. For subtle color variations, select shades from only one card. To create a slightly more dramatic look, choose shades from across one or more cards in the same intensity. Spice up the scheme with a few dashes of another color, perhaps on decorative trims, accessories, or pillows.

Measuring for Window Treatments

Follow the old woodworker's adage—measure twice, cut once—and you're less likely to waste fabric and time.

Whether you plan to purchase ready-made window treatments or make your own, knowing how to measure a window correctly will ultimately save you time and money. Use these tips so all your treatments measure up:

To mount inside window casings: Plan to hang fabric shades and Roman shades inside the casings. Measure from inside jamb to inside jamb and from the bottom of the top casing to the windowsill (A). Not all windows are square, so check these measures in three locations along the frame. Write down the smallest dimension so that the treatments are sure to fit.

To mount outside window casings: Panels, valances, and cafe curtains look best when covering the window framing. Measure from outside edge to outside edge, from side to side and top to bottom (B).

Measuring for tab tops: The secret behind good-looking tab tops is to hang them so the wall—and not the window frame—shows between the tabs. Start by measuring from the top of the window frame to the floor (C); then add 4 to 7 inches so you have enough length to hang the treatments above the frame.

For treatments with rod pockets or pleats: Use the same arrow (C) as a guideline for measuring for rod pocket and pleated panels. This allows you to hang the panels high enough so that pleats and hems won't be visible from outside the house.

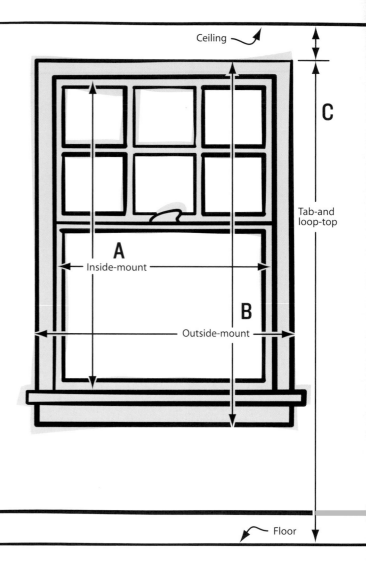

Ceiling

C

Tab-and loop-top

A
Inside-mount

B
Outside-mount

Floor

Have a Seat

Sit on anything. When is a canoe not a canoe? When it's a seat! Frank placed a pillow-filled canoe in a Knoxville: Stubbs Bluff basement for funky seating in a tiki-theme karaoke room. Automotive parts, old machinery, and architectural salvage from auctions and flea markets have also been known to turn up in one-of-a-kind furniture.

Celebrate special spaces. Architecturally interesting spaces—areas under windows, in nooks and crannies, or under sloping rooflines—can be great opportunities for building in custom seating. For example, in Austin: La Costa Drive, Hildi built a low-back, I4-foot sofa to fill a steeply angled nook that could easily have become wasted space.

Make it multifunctional. With careful planning, seating can double as a storage unit, a room divider, a display area, and more. The top of Vern's bench for a Chicago: Fairview Avenue kitchen lifts off for extra storage.

Pay attention to details. If you can't afford the Victorian settee or 1960s mod sectional that your heart desires, consider adding classic details to basic, inexpensive furniture pieces for a custom look. The seat of Edward's elegant chaise longue is a simple padded platform he built, but luxurious black fabric and finials for legs made the piece an attention-grabber.

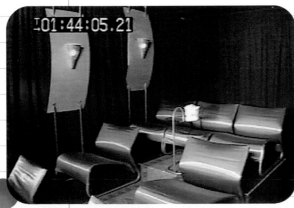

Explore multiple levels. All the seating in a room doesn't have to rest directly on the floor. Place seating on different levels to create conversation clusters or position the seating for specific activities. Doug positioned sleek silver chairs on three platforms of different heights to create stadium-style seating in a home theater in Portland: Everett Street.

117

Before

Except for a fireplace and a trio of stained-glass windows, this room lacked character and featured bowling alley dimensions.

Striped and Stylish

Vern refreshes with white, then excites with color.

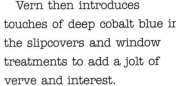

COLOR LESSON: Choose white + a color for elegance.
BACKGROUND: In this Las Vegas family room, bold blue upholstery looks rich against a backdrop of mellow, tone-on-tone stripes. A white armoire helps intensify the blue for an even more opulent look. The result is a classic setting with contemporary accents that wipes away any memories of boring beige.

Creative Contrasts ◀

Whenever you want to make a dramatic yet classic statement, start with a soft backdrop and then add bursts of one color. Using a trio of square stained-glass windows as a guide, Vern painted wide and narrow stripes in two soft colors all around the room, making the lighter color stripes as wide as the windows and the darker stripes about half that width. The treatment helps de-emphasize the length of the room by placing the emphasis on the vertical. It also adds understated beauty and gives the space an airy feel.

Vern then introduces touches of deep cobalt blue in the slipcovers and window treatments to add a jolt of verve and interest.

Fashion Lines ◀

Vern designed a custom-made entertainment armoire for additional storage and a touch of refined style. Open shelves for art and books flank a quartet of doors smartly embellished with thin strips of molding; the molding echoes the shape of the three square windows. White paint makes the piece stand out as another room-refreshing element.

119

"This room is partially inspired by the mother's painting (above the armoire)," Vern says, "but I'm not one to design an entire room around one object. To me, this room is about capturing a summer day.

Top-Notch Transformations ▲

An understated taupe rug helps anchor the seating
arrangement and offers subtle texture and warmth atop
the ceramic tile floor. As a final touch, Vern hung a
painting—done by one homeowner's mother—above the
armoire (see page 119).

Affordable Color ◀

Cobalt blue slipcovers bring new color and life to a pair of old couches, and armloads of pillows promise sink-in comfort as well as more color and a few variations on the stripe theme. The coffee table is actually two thrift store computer desks with shortened legs and fresh paint, positioned side by side. A white, lemon-filled basket and softly glowing votives add warmth to the calm, cool room.

121

Always-Classic Stripes

When you want a pattern that goes with anything, choose stripes. Thick or thin, tall or short—stripes can be either elegant or casual depending on the colors and how you execute the lines.

Elegant	For an elegant look, use tone-on-tone stripes, as Vern did in this room. Or make alternating stripes stand out with a coat of satin or gloss polyurethane.
Contemporary	To create a look that's more modern and clean, use bolder hues and consider the horizontal stripe technique shown on page 42.
Casual	Vertical stripes brushed on freehand (see page 122, D), in any color palette, appear airy and casual. Choose a brighter color palette for a fun treatment in a child's room.
Playful	To bring interest to a large, boxy room, alternate plain and patterned stripes, using the technique on page 122 (A though C).
Show-Stopping	A single wall of stripes sometimes has more dramatic effect than an entire roomful. Choose the wall, select the colors, and prepare for impact!

Although they're easy to create, stripes pack a lot of design power. To paint stripes on the walls of your home, you'll need a pencil, a measuring tape, a carpenter's level, low-tack painter's tape, paintbrushes or rollers, and the paint colors of your choice. To create the moirélike stripe shown here you'll also need an inexpensive combing tool.

A

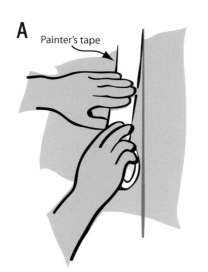

Painter's tape

B

Painter's tape

Paint comb

C

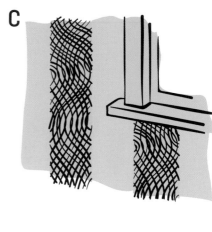

D

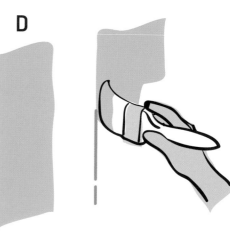

1 Paint the wall with a base coat of color and let dry. Determine the width of the stripes you want. Measure and mark the locations of stripes across the wall. Use a carpenter's level to draw straight vertical lines from the top of the wall to the floor. Align painter's tape along the outside edge of the lines to outline alternating stripes (A).

2 Mix equal portions of latex paint and glazing medium. Paint a stripe with the glaze. Pull the paint comb down through the fresh glaze, making S motions until the stripe is filled (B).

Comb down through the glaze again but reverse the S pattern to create the look of moiré fabric (C). Peel off the tape before the glaze dries.

Variations include painting stripes only above or below a chair rail. Make some stripes shine by brushing on satin or gloss polyurethane over a base coat. Instead of combing, you may want to rag, sponge, stencil, or stamp alternating stripes. To create a more casual, playful wall treatment, paint stripes freehand (D), using only a pencil mark as a guide.

Shredded stripes. Sure, stripes are straight, but they can take any design direction. Consider grouping small sets of stripes at different angles. Laurie made an upholstered headboard with squares of yellow and white striped fabric that alternated, creating a basketweave pattern.

Stripes for depth. Stripes don't have to be a flat, two-dimensional affair. Add texture, pattern, and depth to a design by using thicker materials to create stripes. A California living/dining room got a burst of visual interest when Hildi attached strips of lightly stained 1×2 wooden boards every few inches along the walls.

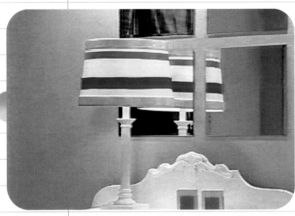

Stripes as accessories. If you're not ready to commit to striped walls or upholstery, experiment with striped designs on inexpensive accessories such as frames, lampshades, pillows, and window treatments. Laurie glued ribbon strips to a basic lampshade and unified the pretty pastel colors in a Boston girls' bedroom.

Stripes as artwork. On a wall or special piece of furniture, a few simple stripes can be a graphic focal point. Bands of color can emphasize the height (if placed vertically) or width (if placed horizontally) of furniture and walls. Doug hung three strips of first-cut poplar on the walls of a Pennsylvania living room as a rustic art installation.

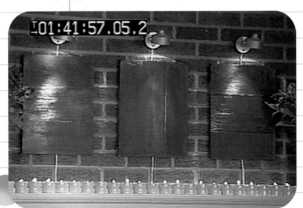

Stripes everywhere! Take stripes to an extreme. Vern went stripe-crazy in a Colorado living room, installing two different shades of laminate flooring, creating stripe artwork, and lining votive candles in a single-file strip above a fireplace.

ENERGIZED
WITH ACCENTS

Chapter 7: Energized with Accents Dollops of accent color—especially bold or unexpected hues like lemon yellow and cotton candy pink on Easter eggs—work with the dominant color to make any room more exciting. See how the *Trading Spaces* crew uses fabric, paint, accessories, and other materials to energize a variety of spaces.

A Lounge for Him

Edward gives diminutive digs lots of verve with purple and black.

COLOR LESSON: Choose dark accent colors for chic looks.
BACKGROUND: Edward didn't let the small size of this room hold him back. He skillfully uses colorful accents in a sleek seating area, a cool window treatment, and a workstation that's as organized as it is good-looking.

A Happenin' Palette for a Happenin' Place ◄

Everyone wants his or her own little corner of the world, and this room brimming with deep, rich accent colors is perfect for Edward's male homeowner. "I made a lounge for him," Edward says. Inspired by the purple and black neck roll pillow, purchased for $12.99, Edward opted for a bold purple ceiling, soft gray walls, and dramatic black accents meant to inspire the homeowner's creative musical talents. As off-the-cuff artwork, two guitars hang on the wall—each framed by floor-to-ceiling, swept-back white fabric panels and spotlighted for display. The conga drum occupies a prominent spot.

The one-of-a-kind window treatment is fabricated from acrylic rectangles cut from a $3 poster frame; some have been spray-painted purple. Bent paper clips link the rectangles so they hang from ceiling to floor. Edward dubs them "stained-glass panels."

For only $1 per yard, gray fabric slipcovers the existing chaise, adapting it to the new color scheme.

Blue Light Special ◄

With everyone looking up at the dramatic purple ceiling, no ordinary light fixture would do. A threesome of halogen pendent lights with bold blue glass shades adds another hip element to the room.

Before

Though small, this room holds promise as an inviting retreat for a guy. Edward pegs the alcove as a spot for a built-in computer desk and shelves.

127

Reuse and Refresh ▲

Scouring the house for unused furniture, Edward came across this coffee table, which had seen better days. A few coats of black paint transformed it into a stylish piece the homeowners hardly recognized. A black-painted frame pulls the armchair into the scheme too.

Work and Play ▶

Though an untrained eye might have seen this alcove as useless, Edward envisioned it as a computer niche. Amy Wynn cut the desk top and shelves to size, and all pieces were painted black to stand out against the purple wall. The vertical dividers angle out, giving the shelf unit a stylish sculptural look.

COLORING LESSONS — An Accent on Black

Black works in virtually any color scheme. Almost any room looks dressier and more put together with some deft touches of black.

To bring more black accents into your home without a lot of effort, paint a few mirror and artwork frames. Brush black on other smaller accessories, such as candlesticks or decorative boxes. Or paint the legs on a dining or coffee table black. Consider a few black-painted pinstripes on cabinet doors or on moldings.

For additional drama, inject larger doses of black in the form of upholstered furniture, window treatments, decorative wall moldings, floorcoverings, bedding, shelving, cabinetry, and more.

If you prefer a rustic look, furniture can still look striking dressed in black. After painting a piece of furniture black and letting it dry, add some vintage appeal and detail by sanding edges, around handles and legs, and anywhere that natural wear might occur.

Fun with Acrylic Sheets

Cuts like wood and paintable too!

Whether clear or tinted, versatile acrylic sheets lend a mod touch to furnishings, walls, window treatments, and more. Slice it into squares, rectangles, or more elaborate shapes with a straightedge and acrylic cutter and bring any item into the 21st century.

You can cut acrylic sheets much like wood, and the pieces can be drilled or joined with glue.

You'll find acrylic in clear sheets and in solid and transparent colors; textures, and patterns are also available (A). Sheets come in several thicknesses and sizes.

Acrylic panels are shape-shifters; they can become almost anything you want:

✱ Panels in cabinet doors. Remove the solid-wood panels from the center of cabinet doors and replace them with clear or colored acrylic sheets cut to fit. For a visual bonus, backlight the panels for a pleasing nighttime glow.

✱ Contemporary frames. Cut two pieces of acrylic to the same size. Drill a hole at each corner, slip artwork between the panels, and secure the panels with screws and nuts or thin pieces of wire.

✱ Decorative boxes. Cut a top, sides, and a bottom to form a box shape using the cutting directions that follow. Then make intricate cutouts in the pieces, using a scroll saw equipped with a blade designed for cutting acrylic. Leave the protective film on the acrylic sheet, apply a layer of duct tape, and glue

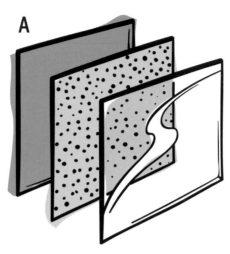

A

your pattern over the duct tape. Follow the outline of the pattern with your scroll saw; then remove the pattern, tape, and protective film. Use small hinges and screws to assemble the box.

✱ Straight cuts. Always leave the plastic film on the acrylic sheet while you make cuts. To make straight cuts, use a handheld tool designed for cutting plastic. Position

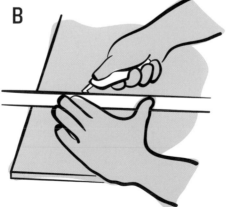

B

a straightedge where you want to cut and score the plastic with the cutting tool (B). Make several passes with the cutting tool to deepen the score line.

Align the score line along a table edge as shown (C) and position the straightedge on top of the sheet so it is aligned with the score line. While pressing down on the straightedge, press downward on the overhanging portion of the sheet. The acrylic will snap along the score line.

A table saw equipped with a blade designed for cutting acrylic will also make straight cuts. When drilling, use only bits designed for acrylic.

After making cuts, lightly sand the cut edge until it's smooth.

To glue acrylic sheets, use solvent cement and clamp or tape the pieces together until dry. Let dry according to manufacturer's directions—usually 24 to 48 hours.

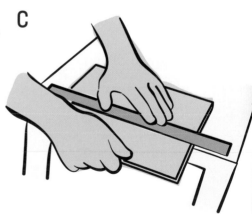

C

You'll find an abundance of acrylic sheets and related supplies available online—plug "acrylic sheets" into any search engine. Locally, check the phone business directory under "Plastics—Rods, Tubes, Sheets."

130

Way-Cool Window Treatments

There must be as many ways to dress a window as there are windows in the world. Here are five favorites from the *Trading Spaces* designers.

Extend a theme. Even window treatments can be part of a decorating theme. Consider utilizing the unusual materials, shapes, and colors that appear throughout a room in the window coverings. In a camouflage-theme living room, Kia's voluminous drapes were made from a parachute.

Seek out unusual fabrics. You don't have to rely solely on fabric stores for interesting materials, designs, and prints. Vintage clothing, table linens, and furniture upholstery can all serve as inspiration for custom window treatments. Gen covered a wooden valance with a white and orange obi in a Seattle living room.

Look beyond fabric. Create stunning window treatments with wood, metal, or plastic—almost any material that you can buy in flat sheets will work. Doug folded lengths of metal screen door mesh like a paper fan and hung them as stationary blinds in a Cincinnati dining room.

Skimp on hardware. Invest limited decorating dollars in higher-quality fabrics rather than expensive hardware. Plan to upgrade hardware later. Edward fashioned rods and finials for an Indianapolis bedroom by covering cardboard tubing and plastic foam balls with brown fabric.

Paint it to perfection. If you find a premade window treatment that suits your style but not your color palette, embellish the treatment with painted details (or repaint the treatment entirely) to coordinate with the room. Doug whitewashed matchstick blinds in a sunroom in Philadelphia: Valley Road.

Before

The owners of this living room love country style and bright colors. Gen is about to clean up the look and layer on a lot more color.

Country Refreshed

Gen uses juicy accents to revive a family room.

COLOR LESSON: Play with your palette for punchy accents.
BACKGROUND: With a nod to the homeowners' love of bright colors and country style, Gen updates casual plaid seating and gives the deep gray walls a jolt with splashy hues that look good enough to eat.

It Pays to Recycle ◄

Some of the most exciting palettes come from toying around with unusual combinations until the look feels right. Peeling raspberry-color slipcovers off the sofa and chair, Gen discovered some downright decent plaid fabric. Handsome gray-green for the walls picks up on the tone of the plaid and offers an understated backdrop for the brighter accent colors. Gen reworked the slipcovers into pillows and an ottoman slipcover. Apple green fabric and paint team up with the bold splashes of raspberry for a complementary pairing that's irresistible. Crisp white balances the bold palette to create a cleaned-up country look that's both casual and sophisticated.

Pillows Aplenty ◄

Colorful fabrics play an important role in the welcoming atmosphere of this room, and armloads of pillows smoothly tie this palette together. For variety, some of the raspberry-color pillows feature a herringbone pattern. Gen added big floor pillows and a rug that perfectly match the walls. At the windows, apple green sateen panels—topped with fabric-covered particleboard cornices—introduce a pleasing touch of sheen into the decor.

Seek out the freshest colors by paying attention to the seasonal items and displays at discount stores, malls, and supermarkets. If a punchy palette catches your eye while shopping, just imagine what it could do in your home.

> "The new hardware is a subtle change," Gen says, "but it speaks loudly when the whole room is put together.

Past Meets Present ▲

After nixing the homeowners' vertical entertainment center, Gen and Amy Wynn decided on this more horizontal version—a series of cubical boxes with doors that are painted white. Punched-aluminum panels (available at home centers and sometimes used to cover radiators) dress up the cabinet doors, creating a look reminiscent of an antique country pie safe. Mounds of fuchsia pillows and bowls of perky green apples toss in punches of the accent color palette. Gen describes the overall look as "something familiar, but a little bit updated."

Traditional-shape table lamps receive a modernized look too, with apple green shades on top and a crisp white finish on the bottom.

Little Cash, Big Splash ▲

Gen applied a coat of white paint and new clean-lined pewter-finish hardware, bringing an existing cherry-stained end table into the new color scheme.

Set the Mood
The psychology behind color choices

Color affects how people feel, so choose your hues carefully to evoke the mood you have in mind. Start by understanding the purpose of the room and how you want people to feel in it. In general, warm colors are sociable; cool colors are private. Everyone has inherent behavioral responses to colors. The more intense the color, the stronger the response. So don't use stimulating bright yellow paint in a room where you want to catch some quality shut-eye. Here's a sampling of how color influences mood:

Blue	Blue is associated with calm, trust, and dependability. It creates a psychologically safe environment in kids' bedrooms. Blue also lowers blood pressure, which makes it an ideal choice for an adult bedroom. It's also effective in study spaces and home offices.
Green	Green is relaxing because it is the easiest color for your eyes to process. Because it sustains concentration, it is the best color for your home office. Now considered a neutral, it blends easily.
Red	Red stimulates conversation and appetite, so it's perfect for a dining room. It's also known to raise blood pressure and energy levels. It can evoke passion, love, lust, and anger.
Yellow	Yellow stimulates memory. It can be uncomfortable to view for long periods of time because it is difficult for your eyes to process. It also clashes with many people's skin tones, so avoid it in the bathroom. Use yellow in the kitchen or as a quick energy boost in a hallway.
Black	Black can be all-consuming—use it carefully. It suggests dramatic sophistication and dignity but also mourning. Grays and blacks can be depressing, so team them with bright colors.

A screen is a great way to introduce more color into a room, camouflage elements you want to hide, serve as an airy room divider, or balance awkward architecture.

Screens, such as the two projects shown here, are especially easy to make and require minimal tools, skills, or investment in time and dollars. Both of these screen styles offer lots of decorative options. Paint or stain the louvered screen in any color and dress it up with stamps, stencils, decorative cording, buttons, or other embellishments. The bifold door screen is equally suited to decorative interpretation. Brighten it with paint or stain, cover it with wallpaper or fabric, or decoupage it with favorite photos or images cut from magazines. Follow these steps to make your own screen:

Multilevel Louvered Screen

Start with three unfinished louvered panels in various heights. You'll also need six double-acting hinges, which are also called swing-clear hinges. These hinges bend in both directions to fold either way and to fold flat for storage.

Clean screens thoroughly with a wire or stiff straw brush if necessary. Sand the screens and wipe debris away with a tack cloth. Brush or spray a coat of clear polyurethane. As the panels dry, periodically move the louvers so they don't stick in one position. After the sealer dries, lightly sand the panels again to smooth the raised grain. For a more refined look, spray paint the shutters with a spray gun or a can of flat spray paint in the desired color, following manufacturer's recommendations.

Position the panels with the tallest one in the center; use chairs or other items to hold them upright. Evenly space three double-acting hinges between each set of panels, carefully aligning the bottoms of the panels. Mark the position of the hinge holes and install the hinges according to the manufacturer's directions. Finish the panels as desired.

Bifold Door Screen

Start with two sets of hollow-core bifold doors. You'll also need three bifold door hinges and No. 4 flathead wood screws for the hinges.

Lay one set of doors on top of the other, carefully aligning the ends and edges. To join the two sets, position an open bifold door hinge 3½ inches from the top of the doors along the edge; screw the hinge to the edges of both doors. Position and fasten a second hinge 3½ inches from the bottom. Center a third hinge between the others. Finish the doors as desired. If you plan to cover the doors with wallpaper, prime the doors first and let dry.

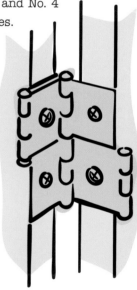

Fabulous Furniture Rescues

After you experience the first thrill of salvaging a piece of furniture and reworking it into something attractive and usable, you'll be hooked.

Refresh with custom hardware. If you like the basic design of a piece, replace dated hardware with new accessories—or consider making hardware yourself from piping, driftwood, wooden utensils, and more. Laurie replaced traditional hardware with pieces of bamboo in a bedroom in Maple Glen: Fiedler Road.

Think outside the home. Great furniture doesn't have to be originally intended for home use; it may have been originally designed for offices, factories, or retail stores. Hildi reupholstered a vintage shampoo chair from an Austin thrift store and placed it in a sewing room as a recliner.

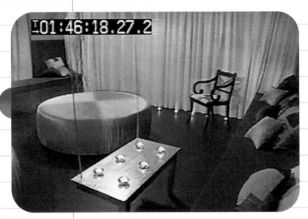

Divide and conquer. Cut apart outdated furniture to save the most-appealing aspects of the piece (great legs, hardwood tabletops). Or cut down oversize pieces to fit into a small room. Doug rescued a coffee table in a Berkeley fraternity house by cutting it in half to make two "hanging tables."

Refresh by recovering. Salvage a piece with great lines by replacing dated, soiled, or damaged fabrics with new upholstery. Look for an introductory furniture upholstery course from a community college or adult education program. Vern reupholstered a thrift store chair with gray wool fabric for a Wake Forest bedroom.

Shake things up. Give new function to a piece of furniture by turning it on its side, upside down, or on its back. Gen turned a bland bookcase on its side and added casters to create a new coffee table in a Cuban-inspired living room in Los Angeles: Willoughby Drive.

Before

This bedroom is too long and narrow, but Edward has some visual tricks up his sleeve.

Paisley Perfection

COLOR LESSON: Pull the perfect accent colors from a piece of fabric.

BACKGROUND: Edward is often drawn to the classics, but here he applies his personal stamp. In this elegant yet energized bedroom, he blows the dust off a traditional paisley pattern and bases the accent colors for the room on a few yards of pricey fabric.

A Narrow Escape ◀

Even with all the special features Edward worked into this challenging space, a "modern traditional" paisley steals the show and sets the right tone for the entire makeover. First, Edward carefully dispersed the fabric throughout the room as elegant bands of pattern. On

the wall shown here, one vertical band serves as a backdrop for a trio of lavender-framed calendar prints. Another paisley band unites the divider wall with the rest of the room.

Faced with an exceptionally long, narrow bedroom, Edward divided the space by adding a partial wall.

Positioned several feet from one end of the room, the divider wall features storage shelves on the side facing the bedroom closet (not shown); on the other side, wall space accommodates a mirror and dresser.

Bathing the room in stately style are two distinctive paint shades: soft gray-blue for the divider and upper perimeter walls and chic China blue for walls below the white-painted chair rail. These subtle shades allow accents of spring green, lavender, and deep purple to take the spotlight. Adding black accent pieces, Edward paints the dresser glossy black, elevating the striking silver pulls to the level of jewelry.

Above the dresser, the mirror with the silver-painted frame slides on a track to reveal the television.

From Bargain to Beauty ◀

Changing a light fixture is one of the simplest ways to give a room a new look. A trip to the salvage yard yielded this chandelier for $15. Strings of pearl beads and a glue gun helped achieve the Cinderella-like transformation.

139

Swirl In Some Color ▲

A line-up of generous pillows covered in paisley fabric soften the headboard area and encourage comfortable reading or working in bed. The paisley also brings eye-pleasing pattern to the tops of the light gray crepe curtain panels.

Edward fashioned the sculpture behind the bed from a corrugated metal window well, painted black on one side and gray on the other. A circular saw was used to

cut the metal into strips, which Edward bent into shapely tendrils that repeat the paisley swirls. Unlike commas and semicolons, pillow accents can go anywhere, but they make a particularly inviting statement when luxuriously piled at the head of the bed. Edward pulled the color scheme together in this one vignette, layering the paisley pillows with deep purple and spring green accent pillows and connecting the pattern to the lush blue bedspread.

Changeable Color

COLORING LESSONS

Got a whim? Swap your color scheme in a wink.

If quick-change accent color is your game, start with neutral furnishings and play with palettes as often as you like using the following elements.

Accessories. Stores are stocked with an unlimited variety of colorful accessories, from decorative boxes and lamps to knickknacks and picture frames.

Artwork. Look for prints or photographs in the colors you love and frame them. Consider budget sources of artwork, such as calendars and bargain-bin art books.

Collections. If you're a collector, take a cue from museums and rotate displays. Pull out some collections for one season and store others until you're ready for a change.

Dishware. Whether you've inherited your grandmother's china or you love acquiring assorted dishes, teacups, or platters from flea markets and antiques malls, dishware brings exciting color and pattern into a room. Display pieces alone or mount them in groupings on a wall.

Duvets. Think of duvets as big pillowcases for comforters. For a small sum, you can slip on a new one anytime.

Flowers. Besides introducing explosions of color to a room, fresh flowers simply "feel" good. Treat yourself as often as you can with beautiful bouquets. Or consider silk substitutes for long-lasting color.

Linens. For the bed or the table, linens come in a plethora of colors and patterns and promise a soft touch for your rooms. Track down affordable linens during white sales; also check flea markets, garage sales, and estate auctions.

Paint. For a powerful transformation, pull out the paint cans and rollers. Enough said.

Pillows. Sprinkle these around with abandon. When you're tired of them, gather them up and stitch new colorful covers. Follow the directions on page 142.

Rugs. Give a neutral carpet a splash of color with a new rug. You'll find a variety of sizes and even playful shapes.

Slipcovers. Even if you don't sew, purchased slipcovers fit and look better than ever before. Change them with the seasons or whenever you tire of the old ones. See page 68 for information on measuring your furnishings for slipcovers.

Throws. A cuddly blanket throw is a wonderful way to warm up a room for fall and winter. Put throws away for a cooler, cleaner look during the fair-weather months.

Window treatments. No-sew fusible webbing and clip-on curtain rings mean that anyone can fashion new fabric panels for windows in a weekend.

Sew-Easy Pillows

If you've ever wanted to try sewing with a machine, pillows are the ideal project for beginners: Stack together two squares of fabric and stitch.

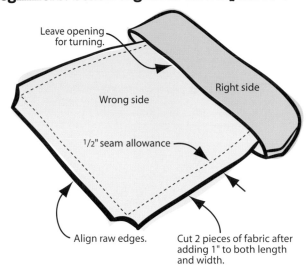

Leave opening for turning.

Right side

Wrong side

½" seam allowance

Align raw edges.

Cut 2 pieces of fabric after adding 1" to both length and width.

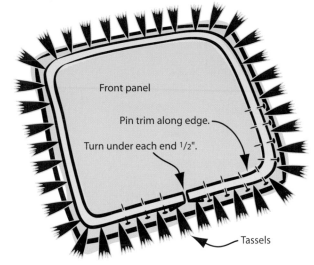

Front panel

Pin trim along edge.

Turn under each end ½".

Tassels

Cut two pieces of fabric that are 1 inch larger all the way around than the pillow form. (Ready-to-cover pillow forms are available at fabric and crafts stores.) Stack the pillow front and back with right sides together and pin to mark the ½-inch seam allowance. Sew around three sides, leaving one end open for turning. Turn right side out; insert the pillow form or stuff with fiberfill batting. Hand-stitch the opening closed.

Fringe Benefits

For variety, add fringe or cording to the perimeter of your pillow. Simply stitch the trim to the right side of the pillow front prior to sewing the front and back together.

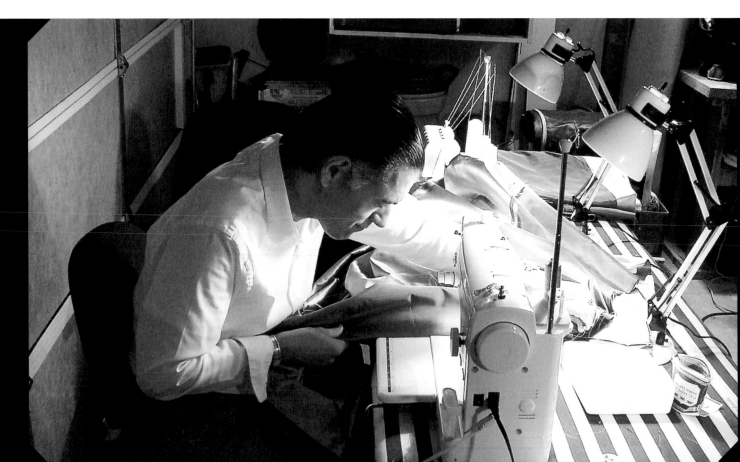

Pillow Pizzazz

Besides being soft and cuddly, accent pillows offer armloads of decorative opportunities. One lowly pillow can accommodate an explosion of color. Consider these notable pillow approaches.

Theme dream. Pillows are a fantastic place to explore a theme. Buy or create pillows that feature extreme color, distinct artwork, or exquisite trimmings. If your tastes change, a new look is only a pillow or two away. Gen embellished blue and pink pillows in a Philadelphia basement as part of her Scrabble-theme rec room.

Here, there, everywhere. Sure, pillows look great on couches and chairs, but empty patches of floor, quiet corners, and even cabinet tops can also benefit from the fluffy effect of a pillow or two. To bring a splash of color to the neutral flooring, Gen sewed two large monogrammed dog pillows out of the same fabric she used for a new bedspread in a San Diego bedroom.

Hang on to a favorite. Stuff and sew closed a favorite fabric memento to create a one-of-a-kind accent pillow/conversation starter. Consider repurposing an old T-shirt, a pair of jeans, a decorative flag, or a canvas schoolbag. Gen selected several woolly shirts and sweaters to convert into lodge-look pillows for a rustic basement den.

Think shapely. Pillows don't have to be square affairs. Round, oblong, and bolster pillow forms are readily available at crafts stores; look for finished pillows at housewares stores. Doug fashioned extra-long bolsters for a sectional couch by wrapping swimming noodles with batting and covering them with upholstery fabric in Houston: Sawdust Street.

DRAMATIC FINALE

Chapter 8: Dramatic Finale Experience the satisfaction of creating a room that elicits oohs and aahs. In this chapter, you'll discover that either subtle or bold colors can work with architecture or special finishes to yield stunning results. Get ready to soak up the praise and bask in the glow of your new, dramatic surroundings.

Before

TCR 01:40.09:08
PLAY   LOCK

146

"Plain and boring"—that's how the homeowners describe their bedroom before Frank comes on the scene. They're hoping for a dramatic makeover with a more romantic look.

Isn't It Romantic?

Frank chooses white for dramatic delights in a master bedroom.

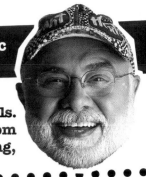

COLOR LESSON: Layer on the white in a room by varying texture and materials.
BACKGROUND: Frank brings intimacy to a high-ceilinged master bedroom with muted green walls and an array of white—in the headboard, bedding, and yards of gauzy fabric.

The Great White Way ◄

White isn't bland when you mix up the textures and materials associated with it. This big bedroom posed a color challenge for Frank as he transformed the space into a romantic retreat. He started with painting the walls soft green to create an air of serenity and intimacy, but it was the addition of white that made all the difference. Yards of ivory chiffon envelop the bed. Stapling the fabric directly to the drywall allows the yardage to gracefully swag from the wall and up to the ceiling. The generous lengths descend past the foot of the bed and puddle decadently on the floor.

Storage and Style ▼

Clutter is hardly conducive to romance. Frank cleaned up the look of the room with this armoire, sized to accommodate the television on top and a chest of drawers below. Stain, rather than paint, introduces the warm color of wood into the setting. Tuxedo-pleated sheers, which Frank found on sale, carry the dreamy ambience to the windows.

Tall Order ▼

Experimenting with something other than a padded headboard, Frank's design matches the scale of the room at an affordable price. Fluted moldings and rosette blocks offer the style- and budget-savvy solution. Painted low-key ivory to continue the dreamy effect and nailed to the wall, the moldings form a graceful downward arc. Rosette blocks cap off all but two lengths of molding—the outermost ones, which climb higher to touch existing lighting sconces.

Three Ways to Crown a Bed

You'll feel like royalty resting under these.

Kings once surrounded their beds with yards of fabric to keep out the cold; but the height of the canopy was all about status, not practicality. You'll feel royal, and romantic too, in a bed that boasts privacy and elegant style.

These fabric toppers are easy to re-create in the bedroom:

1 Rings of Romance. Towel rings attached to the ceiling allow you to sweep fabric from ring to ring above the head of the bed. Use a drill to make pilot holes, and check that screws are fitted with suitable anchors, such as a hollow-wall anchor or molly bolt, to hold both the fabric and ring.

2 Soft Swags. Drape a length of fabric over brackets you make from PVC pipes and caps. Start by marking where you want the brackets on the wall, using the illustration, *right,* as a guide. For each bracket, screw a white metal flange to the wall at one of the marks, and glue one end of an 18-inch piece of PVC into a threaded plug that fits the flange. Glue a PVC cap to the opposite end of the pipe. Screw the pipe into the metal flange. Finish by draping the fabric over the brackets.

3 Molding Character. This regal look begins with decorative moldings. Measure and cut lengths of molding to the desired size—either following the outline of the entire bed or creating a half-tester canopy that only crowns the head of the bed. Secure the moldings to the ceiling using 4d or 6d finishing nails. If you don't hit a joist somewhere on each length of molding, use screws and screw-in anchors to carry the weight. Cut and hem fabric to the desired length and staple it to the backs of the molding strips.

Towel ring

Metal flange
PVC pipe
Decorative wood rosette
Threaded plug
Cap
PVC pipe

Finishing nails
Ceiling joists
Molding
Molding
Fabric

More Canopies!

Add a fun, flirty finishing touch to any style bedroom.

Still don't have a canopy into your boudoir? See if any of these *Trading Spaces* strategies from the past stir the romantic within you.

01:46:23.00

The view beyond. Sure, a canopy makes a bed cozy, but what about the room beyond the canopy? Canopies made of light, airy fabrics give sleepers soft views of the rest of the room. Gen added twinkling holiday minilights outside a canopy in San Diego: Elm Ridge, to scintillating effect.

01:41:56.07

Fresh interpretation. The mere suggestion of a canopy—a piece of fabric attached to the area above where you sleep—can give the stylish effect of a new piece of furniture. Hildi connected two strips of white lace to the central angle of a cathedral ceiling, allowing an abstract fabric canopy to drape down on the bed.

01:40:40.05.2

Flexible effects. Canopies don't have to be permanent. A custom canopy added above a bed allows you to change or update the look of your bed later. Laurie rested a canopy frame on top of a Queen Anne four-poster bed without destroying the integrity of the structure in New Jersey: Perth Road.

01:41:22.01

Historical influences. Sleeping styles have evolved over the ages. Do some research of furniture designs (a visit to a library or bookstore will yield a world of great examples) and imitate a look you like. By adding a French tester-style canopy to a California bedroom, Laurie gave the room a romantic, historical look.

01:44:26.22.2

More than a bed topper. Enjoy the intimate qualities of a canopy in nonsleeping areas of your home. A canopy can make a great addition to a relaxing reading spot or a festive outdoor dining area. Hildi took canopies to the extreme when she tented an entire Seattle basement TV room in magenta and taupe fabric.

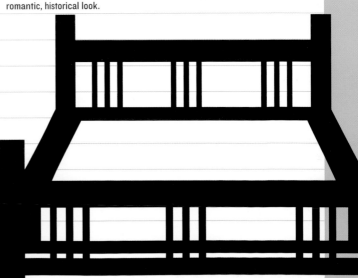

Before

When talking about the old family room, the homeowner points out her love of red and says it would be wonderful if the new room could be happy, bold, and elegant.

Rich in Wood, Gold, and Red

COLOR LESSON: For show-stopping results, choose rich, luxurious materials and finishes for every surface in a space.
BACKGROUND: Three special finishes—wood veneer wallpaper, gold leaf, and lush velvet—yield impressive results for this family room by Vern. Liberal dollops of red make the room seem even warmer and richer.

Smart Color Shopping ◀

Sometimes the best color schemes come together when you find the most luxurious examples of a favorite color (a few lucky finds help too!). For example, Vern enlivened this living room by building on the homeowner's fondness for red. Challenged by a large room in need of seating— only the chaise longue is a keeper—Vern shopped diligently and landed a beefy chair and a sleeper sofa in beautiful brown tones. The same trip yielded one of the most striking additions to the room: wood veneer wallpaper.

Goodbye Fan ◀

In the tradition of many *Trading Spaces* episodes, the ceiling fan came down. However, something stunning took its place: a lovely five-arm black metal chandelier with gold pleated shades. Touches of gold here and elsewhere in the room add glimmer, warmth, and luxury.

Screen Star ◀

To divide the family room from an adjoining dining area, Vern used a four-panel screen, which is custom-made from MDF and embellished with gold leaf centers and deep red borders. Using low-tack painter's tape helps achieve clean edges for each gold leaf panel.

151

Marquetry Magic ▶

Wood veneer wallcovering? Vern discovered this striking marquetry pattern and stayed within the budget by using it on one wall only. "I've never done wallpaper and never thought I would," says a surprised Vern. "It really makes the room dramatic and wonderful and warm."

Lounge Act ▲

Both the existing chaise longue and the entertainment center stayed in the room. A new slipcover in golden brown and red connects the chaise with the palette.

Paring Down ▲

Though wood is a wonderful addition to almost any color scheme, it's possible to have too much of a good thing. Originally, the dark wood entertainment center featured two large sections. Vern separated the pieces, leaving one on this wall so the bulky furniture pair wouldn't distract the eye from the beauty of the wallcovering.

Chic Panels ▲

Vern surprises homeowners and viewers alike with what he can achieve with a few yards of cotton and velvet. For this room transformation, he pairs these fabrics—both in rich shades of red—as simple banded panels. The panels hang ceiling-to-floor on simple silver rods and help unite a trio of windows.

Unadorned, the couch and chair lacked interest. Pillows in red and gold silk, banded in deep red velvet, definitely spice up things, providing a warm look and sink-in comfort.

154.

The Grand Finale ▲

A bold red-painted coffee table with an inset banded in gold leaf serves all the seating at the center of the room and offers a dramatic central focal point. Votive candles light up the recessed center, and shelves underneath provide storage.

> "She loves red, so we introduced it dramatically through the drapery," Vern says. "Then we tied the draperies into these beautiful pillows.

COLORING LESSONS

Tone Up with Wood

Whenever you want a warm look, add wood.

The beauty of wood is its warm color and its versatility. Wood works with any colors you want to use and makes any room more welcoming. To include wood in your decor, use these strategies:

Furniture. From all-wood armoires to wood-frame seating pieces to coffee tables, attractive wood pieces are available at affordable prices. Not all your wood furniture has to match; a variety of wood tones creates a custom color palette all its own.

Floor. If a wood floor isn't in your budget, consider using laminate products that mimic the real thing. Or consider a band of wood flooring around the perimeter of the room, with a carpet inset.

Ceiling. Attaching wood planks or panels (such as beaded board) is one way to gain a wood ceiling. Consider wood beams for a more traditional look.

Walls. Wood veneer wallcovering is one way to go. Alternatively, purchase sheets of wood veneer plywood and secure those to the wall; cover the entire wall or create wainscoting. Add moldings for more depth and use stain to create a library look.

Accessories. From frames to boxes, wood accessories abound. Look for objects made of exotic woods with unusual grains or carved patterns.

155

Metallic Leafing

Love a totally glam look? You can save a bundle by realizing that all that glitters could be gold leafing.

Metallic paints can be beautiful, but look at the special sheen that metallic leaf offers. Vern opted for imitation gold leaf for this room—the real stuff can be pricey. You may opt for other types of metallic leaf, such as silver, aluminum, and copper.

Sizing

Picture frame

Gold leaf

Sponge

1 **Before applying gold leaf,** clean the surface you plan to decorate. Brush on metallic leaf adhesive size, which prepares the surface and holds the leaf in place. Let dry until tacky. The size turns from milky to clear and is very sticky when ready for the leaf.

2 **Transfer the leaf** to the sized surface. Leaf is delicate and can break from careless handling; use the tissue paper between sheets to help transfer the leaf to the size-covered area.

3 **Use a very soft brush** to dab the leaf into place. The leaf sticks only to the sized area. Gently brush away excess leaf. Use the scraps to fill in any areas you missed.

4 **Protect the metallic leaf** with one or two coats of clear satin polyurethane.

Metallic Magic

**Striking silver... Glittering gold...
Pretty pewter... Bold bronze...**

Metals bring their own special quality of color and shine to a room; almost any space can benefit from the addition of some type of metal accent or surface.

Work with what you have. Many rooms have metal accents that have become corroded, tarnished, or dirty over time. Shine metal windows, vents, light fixtures, and more with commercial cleaners. After Gen and Paige spent hours polishing the dingy copper stove hood in a Long Island kitchen, the newly shined fixture became the focal point of the room.

Visit a home center. Inexpensive metal products such as trim, flashing, ductwork, and more are available in a variety of finishes at hardware stores and home centers. Use adhesive or metal fasteners to attach pieces to walls, trim, and furnishings. Frank wove strips of silver flashing to cover a wall in an Oregon dining room and used small silver nails to hold it all in place.

Get luxury for less. Metallic paints are generally inexpensive, but the look of metal can come in even cheaper form. Hildi glued small squares of aluminum foil to a tray ceiling in an Orlando bedroom, creating an elegant inset.

Make metal surfaces, um, metallic. Many metal elements in your home are probably covered with a coat of paint. Rather than removing the paint, apply another coat in a bright metallic shade. Laurie repainted a blah white stove in San Diego with silver appliance paint to stunning effect.

Look up. Ceilings offer large canvases for experimenting with special paint treatments. Introducing metallic accents and trim or covering the ceiling surface with a layer of metallic paint is an ideal way to draw eyes upward. Gen painted a cathedral ceiling in a Maryland bedroom with several layers of metallic gold paint.

episode guide

Think you're the ultimate *Trading Spaces* fan? Prove it by rating the room redos of every episode of the show in this handy-dandy listing guide.

This complete, chronological tour through the years with your favorite decorating show is so chock-full of facts, figures, and funnies that even die-hard fans will learn a thing or two! Check out the Icon Legend below to help locate episodes with High Stress Alerts, Tearjerker Reactions, and more. And don't forget to record your opinion of each and every transformation by using the super-easy ☺ ☺ ☹ Smiley Face scale.

● ☀ = Demolition   ☹ = Tearjerker   ✳ = Ceiling Fan   😬 = Stress Alert   🔫 = Homeowners with Power Tools
🖌 = Paint Explosion   ? = What Were They Thinking?   ⬤◀ = Carpenter to the Rescue $ = Budget Crisis   ♥ = Fan Favorite

Season 1

Knoxville: Fourth & Gill
Cast: Alex, Frank, Laurie, Amy Wynn

The Rooms: In the premiere episode, Frank brightens a den by using a faux-suede finish in shades of gold on the walls, reupholstering the homeowners' Arts and Crafts furniture, and painting two armoires in shades of red, gold, and black. Laurie punches up a bland kitchen by painting the walls electric pear, retiling the floor in large black and white checks, and using chrome accents. She also creates an organized family message and filing center.

Watch For: Frank demonstrates the "Frank Droop," meant to keep your arm from getting tired while painting. (It's a shoulder shimmy crossed with a slight back bend.)

Budget Note: Both Frank and Laurie are under budget, but host Alex never even mentions the fact during the end Designer Chat segment.

Frank's Room: ☺ ☺ ☹
Laurie's Room: ☺ ☺ ☹

Knoxville: Forest Glen ☹ 😬
Cast: Alex, Doug, Hildi, Amy Wynn

The Rooms: Doug creates a romantic bedroom, which he titles "Country Urbane," by painting the walls sage green, building an upholstered bed, pickling an existing vanity, and making a privacy screen. Hildi designs a sleek living room, painting the walls a dark putty, sewing white slipcovers and curtains, hanging spotlights on the walls to showcase the homeowners' art, and building end tables that spin on lazy Susans.

Fashion Report: Doug wears dark, angular glasses and has curly hair.

Notable: On his first episode, Doug throws a couple of low-voltage diva fits: one in which he paces and repeatedly mumbles "Why stress tomorrow when you can stress today?" and another in which he walks off-camera and screams.

Crisis: Hildi creates controversy by wanting to paint a thin black stripe around the edge of the wood floor. Her homeowners hate the idea and refuse to take any part in it. She and Alex eventually do it.

Reveal-ing Moment: One of the living room homeowners starts to cry unhappy tears and exclaims, "Oh my God! They painted my floor!"

Doug's Room: ☺ ☺ ☹
Hildi's Room: ☺ ☺ ☹

Athens: County Road ☹ ✳
Cast: Alex, Frank, Hildi, Amy Wynn

The Rooms: Frank brightens a child's room by painting the walls lavender, hanging a swing from the ceiling, making a wall-size art area with chalkboard spray paint, and spray-painting a mural of white trees. Hildi updates a kitchen/living room area by painting the dark wood paneling and ceiling ecru, hanging cream draperies, slipcovering chairs with monkey-print fabric, building shelves to showcase the homeowners' pewter collection, and painting several pieces of furniture black.

Safety First: When Frank's female homeowner won't tie her hair back while spackling, he tells her that his hair is gone because of a bad spackling incident.

Hurry Up!: Frank falls way behind on Day 2, so Alex takes the AlexCam to a retirement community and gets shots of seniors saying that they've heard Frank might not finish on time.

Quotable Quote: One of Hildi's homeowners must not know her very well; she tells Hildi, "You could've lived in pioneer times."

Frank's Room: ☺ ☺ ☹
Hildi's Room: ☺ ☺ ☹

Alpharetta: Providence Oaks
Cast: Alex, Hildi, Roderick, Amy Wynn

The Rooms: Hildi re-creates a dining room using the existing dining table, aubergine paint, pistachio curtains, two-tone slipcovers, a striking star-shape light fixture, and a privacy screen. Roderick brightens a den/guest room by painting off-white stripes on the existing khaki walls, stenciling a sun motif in a deep rust-red, slipcovering the furniture with an off-white fabric, and installing a wall-length desk that can be hidden with curtains.

Yucky Moment: Amy Wynn holds a pencil between her toes while measuring out the desk unit with Roderick.

Time Waster: Hildi, Alex, and Hildi's homeowners search for two days to find china—digging in the attic and asking the other homeowners where they store it—so they can set the table for the end shot. They never find it.

Notable: Although he's never seen again on the show, Roderick is the first designer to use the term "homework" while talking to the homeowners about what needs to be done before the next morning. However, this is not the standard "homework assignment" scene that appears in later episodes.

Hildi's Room: ☺ ☺ ☹
Roderick's Room: ☺ ☺ ☹

Lawrenceville: Pine Lane ●☀ 🔫 ☹
Cast: Alex, Dez, Hildi, Amy Wynn

The Rooms: Dez adds a feminine touch to a dark wood-paneled living room by whitewashing the walls, painting the fireplace, and dismantling a banister. She finds new ways to display the husband's taxidermy and decoy duck collection, including creating a custom duck lamp. Hildi brings the outdoors in, creating an organically hip living room with a tree limb valance, wicker furniture, minty-white walls, and an armoire covered with dried leaves.

Paint Problems: One of Dez's homeowners apparently spends both days priming and painting one built-in bookcase. His excuse: "Paint dries on its own time."

Wonder Woman: Amy Wynn demolishes Dez's banister seemingly with her bare hands.

Notable: Hildi offers a tired Dez some advice at the end of Day 1: "Delegate, delegate, delegate."

Dez's Room: ☺ ☺ ☹
Hildi's Room: ☺ ☺ ☹

Buckhead: Canter Road ●☀
Cast: Alex, Genevieve, Laurie, Amy Wynn

The Rooms: Gen gets wild in a kitchen by painting the walls electric pear, adding silver accents, using colanders as light covers, and removing cabinet doors. Laurie creates a crisp living room by painting the walls chocolate brown, laying a sea-grass rug, and adding cream and white slipcovers and curtains.

Fashion Report: Gen is barefoot the entire episode.

Quotable Quote: Gen wants to change the flooring but doesn't have time. She expresses her disappointment by saying, "Linoleum bites."

Notable: The now famous "Carpenter Consult" scene debuts, with Laurie consulting Amy Wynn.

Gen's Room: ☺ 😐 ☹
Laurie's Room: ☺ 😐 ☹

Washington, DC: Cleveland Park ⑦ ⊣▮▊

Cast: Alex, Dez, Doug, Ty

The Rooms: Dez creates a funky-festive living room by combining electric pear, white, gray, black, and red paint in solids, stripes, polka dots, and textured faux finishes. Doug goes retro in a basement by making a beanbag sofa and a kidney-shape coffee table and painting the walls bright orange.

Notable: One of Dez's young female homeowners is smitten with Ty and quickly volunteers to work with him on a project, leaving the remaining partner to say to Dez, "Who does she think she's kidding?"

Quotable Quote: One of Doug's homeowners criticizes Doug's free-form planning by saying, "I wish you spent as much time laying this project out as you did on your hair this morning."

Dez's Room: ☺ 😐 ☹
Doug's Room: ☺ 😐 ☹

Alexandria: Riefton Court

Cast: Alex, Frank, Genevieve, Ty

The Rooms: Frank cozies a country kitchen by creating a picket-fence shelving unit and using seven pastel paint colors to create a hand-painted quilt. Gen goes graphic in a living room, blowing up and recropping family photos, turning an existing entertainment center on its side, and painting the walls bright red.

Quotable Quote: Explaining his design, Frank says, "I thought...country quilt. This looks like a quilt threw up in here, but when you see the result, you're gonna love it."

Conflict: Frank questions why Ty is spending more time on Gen's project and less time on the "quilt": "Could it be because [at] the other house the individual is very tall, very gorgeous, and has enough sex appeal to knock over a troupe?"

Frank's Room: ☺ 😐 ☹
Gen's Room: ☺ 😐 ☹

Annapolis: Fox Hollow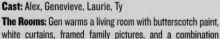

Cast: Alex, Genevieve, Laurie, Ty

The Rooms: Gen warms a living room with butterscotch paint, white curtains, framed family pictures, and a combination wood/carpet floor. Laurie cleans a drab kitchen with muted pumpkin paint, new light fixtures, and a custom pot hanger.

Notable: Gen leads morning stretches with her homeowners before getting to work on Day 2. Laurie removes her first ceiling fan on the show.

Gen's Room: ☺ 😐 ☹
Laurie's Room: ☺ 😐 ☹

Philadelphia: Strathmore Road

Cast: Alex, Frank, Dez, Amy Wynn

The Rooms: Frank goes earthy by painting a living room brown with a sueding technique. He also creates a window seat with storage, handmade accents, and a child-size tepee. Dez tries for "casual elegance" in a living room, using purple paint, a repeated gray harlequin pattern on the walls, and an end table lamp made out of a trash can.

Quotable Quotes: Frank trying to figure out how comfortable a cushion is: "What's the heinie quotient on that?" Frank running out of time on Day 2: "I'm so tense...you could literally use me as a paper press."

Oops!: Frank is 23 cents over budget.

Reveal-ing Moment: The homeowners hate Dez's room with a vengeance, stating "We've got the set of *The Dating*

Game on our walls" and "Beetlejuice lives here."

Frank's Room: ☺ 😐 ☹
Dez's Room: ☺ 😐 ☹

Philadelphia: Valley Road

Cast: Alex, Doug, Laurie, Amy Wynn

The Rooms: Doug softens a sunroom he names "Blue Lagoon" by painting the walls a deep robin's egg blue, painting blue and white diamonds on the hardwood floor, hanging whitewashed bamboo blinds, and adding pale yellow accents. Laurie goes Greek, painting a living room deep russet with black and white accents, adding white Grecian urns, and creating a white bust using one of her homeowners as a model.

Yucky Moment: Doug uses picture wire as dental floss.

Notable: Laurie thinks she's so ahead of schedule on Day 1 that she leads Doug to believe she's been asked to slow down and relax with the family dog so as not to finish too early. She then falls quite behind on Day 2 and becomes very stressed about finishing.

Doug's Room: ☺ 😐 ☹
Laurie's Room: ☺ 😐 ☹

Philadelphia: Galahad Road

Cast: Alex, Hildi, Genevieve, Amy Wynn

The Rooms: Hildi warms a family-friendly living/dining room by introducing coffee-color walls, a midnight blue fireplace, a custom-built sectional couch, and zebra-stripe dining chair covers. Gen brightens a basement den by painting the walls lily pad green, adding orange accents, installing a white modern couch, and weaving white fabric on the ceiling to cover the drop-ceiling tiles.

Fashion Report: Gen wears a cowboy hat the entire episode.

Wise Wynn: Gen plans to demolish an entire wall, but Amy Wynn talks her out of it due to structural concerns.

Wicked Wynn: Amy Wynn tells Alex that the coffee table she's constructing for Gen is "really, really ugly" and that she'd throw it out if it were in her room.

Hildi's Room: ☺ 😐 ☹
Gen's Room: ☺ 😐 ☹

Knoxville: Courtney Oak ✳

Cast: Alex, Frank, Laurie, Amy Wynn

The Rooms: Frank gets in touch with his "inner child" by painting the walls of a basement light denim blue, free-handing murals of trees and flowers, and spray-painting fluffy white clouds. Laurie goes organic by painting a bedroom a deep pistachio green, adding soft draperies, painting a vine around the vanity mirror, and using a cornice board to drape fabric on either side of the headboard.

Fan Debates: Laurie removes another ceiling fan. Alex argues with Frank about his decision to leave two brown ceiling fans in place. Frank defends his choice: "With people dying everywhere and starving children, really, two ceiling fans of the wrong color are minor trivialities."

Quotable Quotes: Frank to Alex: "I would never beat you. You're a nice person, even though you ask some pointed and completely ugly questions."

Frank's Room: ☺ 😐 ☹
Laurie's Room: ☺ 😐 ☹

Cincinnati: Melrose Avenue

Cast: Alex, Hildi, Frank, Ty

The Rooms: Frank adds soft Victorian touches to a living room by exposing the existing wood floor, creating a faux-tin fireplace surround, painting a navy wall border with a rose motif, creating a fireplace screen that matches the border, and building a bench-style coffee table. Hildi gets crafty in a kitchen, creating her own wallpaper with tissue paper and flower stencils. She installs a dishwasher, extends the countertop, builds an island out of the kitchen

---

table, paints the ceiling and the furniture yellow, and lays vinyl tile flooring.

Love Connection?: Frank's male and female homeowners admit to crushes on Alex and Ty, respectively.

Notable: Frank admits to country-and-western dancing with his wife.

Hildi's Room: ☺ 😐 ☹
Frank's Room: ☺ 😐 ☹

Cincinnati: Sturbridge Road ☹

Cast: Alex, Genevieve, Doug, Ty

The Rooms: Gen creates an Indian bedroom for a teenage girl by painting the walls with warm golden and red tones, hanging a beaded curtain, and creating a draped canopy. Doug turns a dining room into a "Zen-Buddhist-Asian room" with a chocolate brown ceiling, warm honey-copper walls, randomly placed Venetian plaster squares, and folded-metal-screen window treatments.

Fashion Report: Gen and her homeowners wear Indian forehead markings on both days for inspiration.

Quotable Quote: Gen calls Doug a "weasel" for usurping some of her lumber and states, "I think he's feeling insecure about his room or he's got a little crush on me and he's just really sad about the rejection."

Scary Stuff: Doug raps.

Notable: Doug gives the first official homework assignment on the show.

Gen's Room: ☺ 😐 ☹
Doug's Room: ☺ 😐 ☹

Cincinnati: Madison & Forest ☹

Cast: Alex, Doug, Laurie, Ty

The Rooms: Doug transforms a Victorian living room into an industrial loft with multiple shades of purple paint, a yellow ceiling, custom art made from coordinating paint chips, wall sconces made of candy dishes, and a chair reupholstered in Holstein fabric. Laurie warms a tiny bedroom with mustard yellow paint, a custom-built entertainment center, and a short suspended bed canopy.

Hurry Up!: Doug has his homeowners create art projects in a 10-minute time frame. Alex walks around with a stopwatch.

Doug's Room: ☺ 😐 ☹
Laurie's Room: ☺ 😐 ☹

San Diego: Elm Ridge 💲 ⑦ ♥

Cast: Alex, Genevieve, Hildi, Amy Wynn

The Rooms: In this infamous episode, Gen truly brings the outdoors in: She covers a bedroom wall with Oregon moss, lays a natural-tone tile floor, and adds a canopy that is lit from above with twinkling lights. Hildi works to convince her homeowners that they can brighten a bedroom by painting the walls and furniture black, adding zebra-stripe floor cubes, and using exposed subflooring in place of carpet.

Un-bear-able: One of Gen's male homeowners constantly carries around a teddy bear.

Yucky Moment: One of Gen's homeowners complains that the moss wall "smells like somebody's old underwear."

Tile Hell: Due to time constraints, Gen chooses to lay floor tiles with liquid nails instead of adhesive and grout. Her team ends up re-laying many tiles during Day 2 because the adhesive doesn't quite work. Hildi's grout unexpectedly dries white and looks terrible next to dark concrete tiles. Hildi improvises by going over budget and buying rugs.

Busted: Hildi creates a copper mesh bust using herself as a model. The female homeowner isn't thrilled with the idea and says, "You went to design school?"

Gen's Room: ☺ 😐 ☹
Hildi's Room: ☺ 😐 ☹

159

San Diego: Hermes Avenue

Cast: Alex, Laurie, Genevieve, Amy Wynn

The Rooms: Laurie brightens a kitchen by painting the walls Tiffany-box blue, hanging butter yellow draperies, building a banquette seating area, coating the stove in chrome-colored paint, and painting the cabinets butter yellow. Gen uses Georgia O'Keeffe's Southwestern paintings as inspiration for transforming a living room. She paints the walls clay red, hangs a cow skull above the fireplace, adds a woven rug, hangs new light fixtures, frames large black and white cropped photos of the homeowners' children, builds a distressed coffee table with firewood legs, and covers the existing baby bumpers with crafts fur.

Oops!: Gen accidentally steps into a bucket full of spackling compound and must hop around on one foot until one of her homeowners brings her a towel.

Budget Buster: Laurie can't afford to spend money on cabinet hardware, so her homeowners ask for permission to buy it themselves as a gift for their friends. Laurie agrees. During Designer Chat, Alex says that she'll bend the rules once for Laurie, but never again.

Reveal-ing Moment: The female living room homeowner is so excited about her room that she picks up Alex—twice.

Laurie's Room: ☺ ☺ ☹
Gen's Room: ☺ ☺ ☹

San Diego: Wilbur Street

Cast: Alex, Frank, Doug, Amy Wynn

The Rooms: Frank mixes British Colonial and tropical looks in a living room using soft mauve paint, exposed wood flooring, several flowerpots and vases, and a custom architectural piece. Doug updates a dark kitchen with a "Tuscan Today" theme, using Venetian plaster tinted "Tuscan Mango" (OK, it's orange), painting the cabinets white and orange, and installing wood flooring.

Quotable Quotes: Frank-isms abound in this episode. Frank on his wall hanging: "OK, now we're gonna make a metal taco." Frank on how tired he feels: "If someone invited me out to dinner, I'd have to hire someone to chew my food." And Frank on his finished room: "You could get malaria in this room it's so tropical."

Ouch!: Alex helps Frank hot-glue moss to flowerpots and manages to lay her entire palm on a freshly glued spot. She gets hot glue and moss stuck to her hand, and Frank runs off to find first aid.

Frank's Room: ☺ ☺ ☹
Doug's Room: ☺ ☺ ☹

Knoxville: Stubbs Bluff

Cast: Alex, Frank, Doug, Ty

The Rooms: Doug brings a farmhouse kitchen up-to-date by painting the walls a muted coffee color, adding sage and lilac accents, building benches in the dining area, painting the cabinets, and laying vinyl tile. Frank lets the ideas flow while punching up a basement with a karaoke stage, a tiki hut bar, and several other tropical accents—including a canoe for seating.

Oops!: Even though Doug and Alex spend much of the episode mixing plaster to coat a shovel and a pitchfork to hang on the wall, the plaster won't dry fast enough, so Doug ends up spray-painting the tools instead.

Fashion Report: Frank wears a hula outfit—complete with coconut bra—and asks, "Am I showing too much cleavage?"

Quotable Quote: Frank disses Ty's mellow attitude, saying "He goes through like life's little pixie, like a little gnome looking for a mushroom."

Yucky Moment: Frank gnaws off a tree branch with his teeth.

Frank's Room: ☺ ☺ ☹
Doug's Room: ☺ ☺ ☹

Miami: 168th/83rd Streets

Cast: Alex, Laurie, Dez, Ty

The Rooms: Laurie warms up a living room by painting the walls brick red with black and cream accents, building two large bookcases, hanging botanical prints, slipcovering the existing furniture, and using a faux-tortoiseshell finish on a coffee table. Dez adds drama to a bedroom by applying a "pan-Asian ethnic theme" featuring upholstered cornice boards, mosquito netting, and stenciled dragon lampshades.

Conflict: Laurie's homeowners want to install a faux fireplace, and she vetoes it. The homeowners convince Ty to help them build a square frame and paint logs and a fire on it. They keep putting it in the room, and Laurie keeps removing it.

Notable: Dez falls ill with the flu on Day 2 and spends a lot of time sleeping on a couch. As a result, her team falls behind. Ty jumps in to help finish the room on time.

Fashion Report: Dez wears an amazing large-brimmed hat during Designer Chat. It features black and white spots, fuzzy black trim, and a very tall white feather. She's outdone herself.

Laurie's Room: ☺ ☺ ☹
Dez's Room: ☺ ☺ ☹

Fort Lauderdale: 59th Street

Cast: Alex, Frank, Hildi, Ty

The Rooms: Frank adds "comfortable drama" to a living room, with bright orange textured walls, a mosaic-top coffee table, slipcovered furniture, and a large custom art project. Hildi goes retro in a Fiestaware collector's kitchen by building an acrylic table, adding period chairs, and hanging large globe light fixtures. She also installs a shelving unit to display the homeowner's collection.

Quotable Quote: Frank describes his coffee table design to Ty by saying, "If you were in Pompeii just before Vesuvius erupted and you grabbed a piece of furniture, it would be this table."

Notable: Hildi removes her first ceiling fan.

Fashion Report: Hildi wears a bikini top during the opening segment.

Frank's Room: ☺ ☺ ☹
Hildi's Room: ☺ ☺ ☹

Key West: Elizabeth Street

Cast: Alex, Frank, Genevieve, Ty

The Rooms: Frank adds a Caribbean touch to a living room by painting the walls light blue, adding a hand-painted mermaid, building a telephone table, and laying vinyl tiles. Gen makes a tiny living room appear larger with her "Caribbean Chill" design, which includes magenta walls with lime green accents, a large custom-built sectional sofa, and a wall decoupaged with pages torn from a 100-year-old book.

Conflict: Frank's homeowners take the reins and wind up running the show. (They also bring a blender with them, because they never travel without it.) They don't finish their homework, claiming a neighbor came over with champagne.

Quotable Quote: Frank describes the shifting control of the project as "Bad reception—it goes in and out."

Frank's Room: ☺ ☺ ☹
Gen's Room: ☺ ☺ ☹

Austin: Wycliff ⑤ 🔌 👶

Cast: Alex, Doug, Hildi, Amy Wynn

The Rooms: Doug creates a funky kitchen by painting the cabinets with blue and purple swirls, extending the existing countertop, applying blue and purple vinyl squares on the wall, and hanging numerous clocks (he titles the room "Time Flies"). Hildi adds drama to a dining room by covering the walls with brown felt, papering the ceiling with small, individual red and gold squares, covering the back of an armoire with dried bamboo leaves, and making custom light fixtures.

Time Flies: Doug covers a wall with clocks set for different time zones around the world. When the homeowner asks where the clock batteries are, Doug realizes that he forgot to buy them and that he doesn't have money left to get any.

Oops!: In order to paper the ceiling, one of Hildi's homeowners uses a pneumatic glue sprayer and accidentally glues his mask to his beard.

Doug's Room: ☺ ☺ ☹
Hildi's Room: ☺ ☺ ☹

Austin: Wing Road 💣 ✳

Cast: Alex, Genevieve, Hildi, Amy Wynn

The Rooms: Gen goes south of the border in a kitchen by adding a mosaic tile backsplash, covering the cabinet door insets with textured tin, painting the floors terra-cotta, and painting the walls yellow. Hildi brightens a living room by applying a textured glaze over the existing gold paint, covering a wall in wooden squares, sewing silver slipcovers, and adding a cowhide rug.

Love Notes: Gen's male homeowner has a crush on Amy Wynn.

Fashion Report: Amy Wynn wears two braids à la Laura Ingalls Wilder.

Gen's Room: ☺ ☺ ☹
Hildi's Room: ☺ ☺ ☹

Austin: Birdhouse Drive

Cast: Alex, Frank, Laurie, Amy Wynn

The Rooms: Frank enlivens a living room by painting three walls sage green, painting the fireplace wall shocking pink, installing floor-to-ceiling shelving on either side of the fireplace, adding a hand-painted checkerboard table, and making unique art pieces. Laurie divides a living/dining room with a suspended piece of fabric, paints the rooms with warm oranges and yellows, adds olive green accents, builds a bench seat, and creates a custom coffee table.

Quotable Quote: Frank describes a wooden rooster he wants to make as "kind of a Frenchy, Mediterranean slash funk Texas rooster."

Time Crunch: During Designer Chat, Laurie confesses that she was running short on time and that the paint on the bench she and Alex are sitting on is still tacky. Laurie freaks a bit because she thinks she's sticking.

Notable: Day 1 is the anniversary of Frank's homeowners. The husband has flowers delivered to his wife, and Frank stays to do their homework that night so the homeowners can go out and celebrate. Oh, and Amy Wynn plays the saw.

Frank's Room: ☺ ☺ ☹
Laurie's Room: ☺ ☺ ☹

Orlando: Lake Catherine

Cast: Alex, Vern, Hildi, Ty

The Rooms: New guy Vern brings warmth and depth into a wine importer's kitchen by painting the walls with two shades of red, installing a custom-built wine rack, building a new chandelier using 36 wineglasses, and creating a new tabletop. Hildi creates a sleek bedroom with gray walls, an aluminum foil ceiling, gray flannel curtains, bamboo curtain rods, and a black armoire covered in bamboo.

Oops!: One of Vern's homeowners juggles lemons and then breaks the vase he's putting them into.

Quotable Quote: When Ty teases Hildi about using too much hair spray, she responds, "Look who's talking, porcupine!"

Tweet Dreams: Hildi includes a live canary in her design and names the bird "Hildi."

Notable: In Vern's premiere episode, viewers are introduced to his perfectionist side: 1) He gives Ty several architectural drawings for what he wants created in the room. 2) After five coats of paint, he and his homeowners are still painting late on Day 2.

Vern's Room: 😊 😐 ☹
Hildi's Room: 😊 😐 ☹

Orlando: Gotha Furlong

Cast: Alex, Genevieve, Frank, Ty

The Rooms: Gen creates romance in a bedroom by adding a ceiling-height cedar plank headboard, butter yellow paint, throw pillows made from a 1970s tablecloth, and cedar bookshelves. Frank makes a bedroom feel "earthy, arty, and wonderful" by painting the walls tan, adding gauzy white fabric to the four-poster bed, building a cedar window seat with storage drawers, painting a floorcloth, and hand painting batik-print pillows.

Quotable Quote: Frank says, "You'd better get some popcorn and a good attitude, because this is something you wanna write home to your mother about."

Fashion Report: Ty has an especially bad hair day. Frank paints Alex's nails and says that he does the same for his wife all the time.

Gen's Room: 😊 😐 ☹
Frank's Room: 😊 😐 ☹

Orlando: Winterhaven

Cast: Alex, Doug, Laurie, Ty

The Rooms: Laurie perks up a seldom used living room with yellow paint, sheer window treatments, a geometric wall design, and a large ottoman. Doug regresses to his childhood while decorating a boy's bedroom. Doug's design, "Americana Medley," includes red walls, a blue ceiling, stenciled stars and cow prints, a tree limb headboard, and a barn door window treatment.

Mean Streak?: One of Laurie's homeowners is afraid of heights, and Laurie keeps putting him on ladders.

Diva Fit: Doug pouts on the couch because he didn't have his own bedroom growing up.

Quotable Quote: Ty tells Alex that Doug's full name is Douglas "Issues" Wilson.

Doug's Room: 😊 😐 ☹
Laurie's Room: 😊 😐 ☹

Albuquerque: Gloria

Cast: Alex, Hildi, Doug, Ty

The Rooms: Hildi warms up a living room by painting the walls brown and copper, applying yellow fabric paint to the existing furniture, making a curtain rod from copper pipe, and installing an entertainment center. Doug sets sail in a living room ("Wind in Our Sails") by painting the walls slate gray, hanging white curtains, installing a banquette, and suspending a large white canvas from the ceiling.

Notable: Alex sings and plays guitar (badly!) for Doug. Doug responds by singing her a song: "Alex is gonna go places we don't want to go. She's gonna be lonely there, singing her sad, sad songs."

Fashion Report: The female homeowners sport blue and green nail polish and nail art that spells out "Trading Spaces."

Hildi's Room: 😊 😐 ☹
Doug's Room: 😊 😐 ☹

Santa Fe: Felize

Cast: Alex, Genevieve, Vern, Ty

The Rooms: Gen designs a modern Southwestern living room ("Adobe Mod") by adding white paint, a custom-built sofa, woven-rope end tables, and clay jars. Vern creates a calming oasis in a kitchen by painting the walls pale blue, installing a planter of wheat grass, laying parquet floor, hanging mirrors, and applying a stained-glass look to the cabinet doors.

Notable: Gen's homeowners smudge the room with sage after clearing the furniture from the room.

Yuck!: Vern tastes the wheat grass, hates it, and tries to spit it

out. Alex makes a wheat grass smoothie and hates it too.

Gen's Room: 😊 😐 ☹
Vern's Room: 😊 😐 ☹

New Orleans: Jacob Street

Cast: Alex, Laurie, Hildi, Amy Wynn

The Rooms: Laurie connects a kitchen/office/dining/living room, using pale yellow paint on the walls, a 20-foot-long sisal rug, slipcovers, new kitchen storage, and a new furniture arrangement. Hildi modernizes a kitchen by painting the walls pistachio green, laying black vinyl tile, building a new island, and finding new uses for plumbing conduit.

Witchy-Poo: In the spirit of New Orleans, Alex cuts locks of hair from Hildi and Laurie to make voodoo dolls. After making the dolls, Alex sticks each doll in the butt to make the designers hurry up.

Notable: The owners of the multipurpose great-room—both the husband and the wife—cry.

Laurie's Room: 😊 😐 ☹
Hildi's Room: 😊 😐 ☹

New Orleans: Walter Road

Cast: Alex, Genevieve, Frank, Amy Wynn

The Rooms: Gen creates an antique look in a bedroom she titles "Bombay Meets Étouffée." She paints the walls peach and pea green, installs a vintage beaded chandelier, and applies an antique gold finish to cornice boards and bookshelves. Frank updates a kitchen by removing garish wallpaper, coating the walls with textured tan paint, painting cabinet drawers in red and green, coiling copper wire around the existing drawer pulls, and installing a large family bulletin board.

Fashion Report: Gen reveals her numerous fabrics to the homeowners by walking into the room wearing the different cloths around her head, waist, and arms.

Oops!: Frank gets stuck in the pantry while he and his team move the refrigerator; he has to shimmy out a small window.

Huh?: Frank titles his room "Beaver Cleaver Meets George Jetson," but there's no apparent reason why.

Measuring Up: Frank measures a space in a room by lying on the floor and stretching his arms over his head. He tells Amy Wynn the length is "one fat man with arms extended."

Quotable Quote: Frank, on the public's perception of designers: "If somebody tells me that a designer is just this little guy who goes around fluffing flowers, I intend to break every bone in his body and make a lamp out of him."

Gen's Room: 😊 😐 ☹
Frank's Room: 😊 😐 ☹

New Orleans: D'evereaux Street

Cast: Alex, Vern, Genevieve, Amy Wynn

The Rooms: Vern kicks up the style in a boys' bedroom with a black and white soccer theme. He paints the walls black and white, upholsters the headboards, creates two desk stations, suspends soccer balls from the ceiling, and lays a black and white vinyl floor complete with a custom soccer ball medallion. Gen heads back to the 1960s in her "Retro Fly" den/guest room by painting multicolor stripes on the walls, hanging retro light fixtures, slipcovering an existing futon, and separating the desk area from the seating area with a chain-link screen.

Quotable Quote: Vern consults with the younger boy at the start of the show. Scotty tells Vern he wants to become an architect. Vern gives him a high five and tells him that "Architects get all the women."

Mean Streak?: Alex plays soccer with the two little boys and tells them that the girls at school will love the new "girlie bedroom." The boys knock her to the ground.

Notable: Gen and her homeowners have problems finding wall studs. When their electronic stud finder stops working,

they start drilling random holes to find the studs.

Vern's Room: 😊 😐 ☹
Gen's Room: 😊 😐 ☹

New York: Shore Road

Cast: Alex, Genevieve, Dez, Amy Wynn

The Rooms: Gen looks to the East for inspiration on a sun porch and creates a tearoom atmosphere with a new sake bar, a seating area, and several organic accents. Dez gives a living room her version of "country with a French twist" by painting the walls yellow, stenciling fern leaves around the room, slipcovering the existing sofa, adding a planter of grass, and hanging geometric window treatments.

Good-Bye: This is Dez's final appearance on *Trading Spaces*.

Oops!: Attempting to shine the sunporch floor, Alex loses control of an electric floor buffer, screams, and eventually falls to the ground.

Oops! Part 2: As Alex huddles near an outdoor fire to get warm, smoke starts to drift toward her, and something gets in her eye. She turns away and complains of being blinded.

Notable: The sunporch homeowners like their room so much, they dance The Monkey.

Gen's Room: 😊 😐 ☹
Dez's Room: 😊 😐 ☹

New York: Sherwood Drive

Cast: Alex, Vern, Doug, Amy Wynn

The Rooms: Vern creates a serene bedroom by painting the walls lilac blue, making a television cabinet out of picture frames, hanging yards of indigo velvet, installing sconces containing live Beta fish above the bed, and creating a 4-foot wall clock out of candle sconces and battery-operated clock hands. Doug designs a relaxing "Zen-sational" bedroom by hanging grass cloth on the walls, making light fixtures out of Malaysian baskets, hanging a full-length mirror on an angle, and building a 6-foot fountain.

Conflict: Doug's mother-daughter homeowners tell him that they both have dates and need to stop working at 5 p.m. Doug and Alex explain that the homeowners agreed to complete all the work necessary to redo the room when they signed up for the show. The next morning, the homeowners complain to Doug about the hard work they had to do the night before. However, they don't know that Doug stopped by the previous night and found that they had recruited friends to do their homework for them.

Vern's Room: 😊 😐 ☹
Doug's Room: 😊 😐 ☹

New York: Linda Court

Cast: Alex, Doug, Frank, Amy Wynn

The Rooms: Doug creates a Mediterranean-flavored living room by covering the walls in yellow Venetian plaster, making custom lamps, building a large armoire to match an existing one, and weaving strips of wood through metal conduit for a woven-wall effect. Frank also heads to the Mediterranean in a living room, applying a faux finish with three shades of yellow paint, then adding stenciled squares and a faux fresco created from drywall, and gondola-inspired lamps.

Resourceful: Doug's and Frank's designs are so close in concept that Doug sends Alex over to Frank's to borrow some teal and black paint.

Quotable Quote: Alex nags Frank, saying "Time is money!" He responds, "Let me write that down so I can embroider that on a whoopee cushion."

Doug's Room: 😊 😐 ☹
Frank's Room: 😊 😐 ☹

161

New Jersey: Sam Street

Cast: Alex, Laurie, Hildi, Ty

The Rooms: Laurie warms up a dining room with yellow paint, shades of berries and pinks as accents, a custom-built cornice board, and cream paint on the existing furniture. Hildi adds drama and romance to a bedroom by painting the walls a yellowed sage green, bringing in several sage silk fabrics, adding a sofa upholstered in burgundy fabric, extending the existing headboard, and building "pillow pod" seating.

Notable: Ty and Alex spend most of the episode running through the woods looking for the legendary Jersey Devil. Laurie does a very bad approximation of a Jersey accent.

Laurie's Room: ☺ ☺ ☹
Hildi's Room: ☺ ☺ ☹

New Jersey: Lincroft 👶 ✳ ☹

Cast: Alex, Laurie, Doug, Ty

The Rooms: Laurie adds style and function to a small kitchen by laying parquet vinyl flooring, painting the walls an ocher yellow, wall-mounting the microwave oven, painting the cabinets white, and creating a home office/family message center. Doug softens a very red living room by painting the walls sandy taupe, adding wooden strips to accentuate the ceiling height, painting colorful checkerboard designs on coffee tables, sewing several brightly colored rag rugs together to create a large carpet, and designing a wooden candleholder using a rope-and-pulley system.

¿Cómo?: Laurie and Ty try to put together a lighting fixture using directions written in Spanish.

Quotable Quote: When Doug's homeowners express concern about the many different accent colors he's using, he responds by saying, "It's not as obnoxious as it could be."

Notable: Alex decides that Doug isn't working fast enough, so she takes over his lamp project. She starts talking to the camera about the project but can't get her pliers open. Doug (in the background) starts doing Alex's job, introducing the episode. He mispronounces things. They decide to keep their regular jobs.

Laurie's Room: ☺ ☺ ☹
Doug's Room: ☺ ☺ ☹

New Jersey: Lafayette Street ✳

Cast: Alex, Frank, Vern, Ty

The Rooms: Frank adds Victorian elements to a dining/living room by painting the walls pink with burgundy accents, showcasing the homeowners' collection of wooden houses, applying decorative molding to the existing entertainment center, and creating original wall art using basic woodcarving skills. Vern softens a living room, making it baby-friendly. He paints the walls two shades of sage green, builds a large ottoman that doubles as a coffee table, builds a sofa out of a mattress, suspends a mantel for the fireplace, and adds bright blue accents.

Good-Bye: This is Alex's last appearance on *Trading Spaces*.

Swede Thing: Vern attempts to put together an armoire, but the instructions are in Swedish. He convinces Ty to put it together, pointing out that Ty looks more like the man in the illustrations.

Bet Me!: Ty and Alex wager a massage on which designer will finish first. Alex takes Vern, and Ty takes Frank. Both Alex and Ty are underhanded in trying to influence the contest. Ty wins.

Frank's Room: ☺ ☺ ☹
Vern's Room: ☺ ☺ ☹

Season 2

Quakertown: Quaker's Way 👶 ❓ ♥

Cast: Paige, Doug, Hildi, Ty

The Rooms: Doug goes "ball-istic" in a living room, painting the walls lime green, building a custom sofa complete with bowling ball feet, hanging a wall of mirrors, making custom lamps out of gazing balls, and adding brown and blue accents. Hildi introduces viewers to the concept of orthogonal design by painting perpendicular lines on the walls and ceiling of a basement, creating a nine-piece sectional seating area, and screening off a large storage area.

Notable: The Season 2 premiere introduces the graphic opening credits, the outtakes during the end credits, and the *Trading Spaces*/TLC/Banyan Productions trailer outside the carpentry area.

Fashion Report: Ty sports a mustache.

Having a Ball: Doug and Ty steal a gazing ball (for Doug's lamp project) from a neighbor's yard. Ty distracts the neighbor, and Doug runs up and steals the gazing ball. Doug tells Paige during Designer Chat that he returned the stolen ball and purchased similar balls to complete his project.

What Was She Thinking?: Although she knows the homeowners have small children, Hildi makes wall art out of acrylic box frames filled with different types of candy.

Tuneful: Doug plays the sax, Hildi plays the drums, and Ty plays guitar during the opening segment.

Doug's Room: ☺ ☺ ☹
Hildi's Room: ☺ ☺ ☹

New Jersey: Tall Pines Drive 💣 ☹ ⌁

Cast: Paige, Laurie, Vern, Amy Wynn

The Rooms: Laurie experiments with several paint colors in a basement by painting a Matisse-inspired mural. She also makes a chalkboard-top kids' table, installs an art station, creates curtains out of place mats, and hangs louvered panels as a room screen. Vern designs a love nest in a bedroom by hanging brown upholstered wall squares, sewing lush draperies, painting the existing furniture white, installing silver candle chandeliers, and adding new bedside tables.

Yucky Moment: Vern's homeowner loves his design choices so much that she moans as he shows her paint and fabric options.

Notable: A human-size nutcracker named Nutty resides in Laurie's room. Nutty stays in the room during the first half of Day 1, and because one homeowner feels that Nutty is staring at him, he paints over one of Nutty's eyes. Later, Nutty floats on a raft in a swimming pool. He makes a final appearance in the passenger seat of a golf cart driven by Amy Wynn.

Laurie's Room: ☺ ☺ ☹
Vern's Room: ☺ ☺ ☹

Maple Glen: Fiedler Road ✳

Cast: Paige, Laurie, Genevieve, Amy Wynn

The Rooms: Laurie paints the walls of a bedroom celadon green, creates a headboard from white and yellow silk squares, paints the existing furniture white, installs bamboo pieces as door hardware, and converts bamboo place mats into pillow shams. Using lilies as inspiration in a living room, Gen paints the walls a yellowed taupe, builds two new couches and a new coffee table, hangs large black and white family photos, and pins prints of vintage botanical postcards to the wall.

Attitude Check: Laurie repeatedly says she's "in a panic mode" about her room; Gen says she's in a "slo-mo hot zone," meaning that the high room temperature is making her zone out.

Laurie's Room: ☺ ☺ ☹
Gen's Room: ☺ ☺ ☹

Northampton: James Avenue ✳ 🔌

Cast: Paige, Hildi, Frank, Ty

The Rooms: Hildi updates a living room with mustard-gold paint, aubergine curtains, yellow and red tufted pillows, a sisal rug, sunflowers, and a river rock mosaic fireplace. Frank creates a nautical Nantucket theme in a living room by painting the walls pale sage, adding yellow and seafoam green pillows, wrapping rope around the coffee table legs to make the table resemble a pier, and building a dinghy-inspired dog bed.

Oops!: Hildi tries to use an industrial sander/scraper, but it won't turn to the right. Pandemonium breaks out as Hildi, Ty, and the male homeowner attempt to get the scraper to work correctly. Eventually, Ty runs it in left-hand circles while Hildi and the homeowner run around holding the cord to keep it from wrapping around Ty.

Amen: Frank and his homeowners say a prayer to the paint gods, thanking them for their color choice.

Quotable Quote: Frank: "OK, I'll work this in between my tennis match with the royal family and my tanning appointment."

Tool Time: Frank encourages his male homeowner to keep sewing, telling him to think of the machine as another power tool. The homeowner decides to think of it as a jigsaw.

Hildi's Room: ☺ ☺ ☹
Frank's Room: ☺ ☺ ☹

Providence: Phillips Street ✳

Cast: Paige, Hildi, Vern, Amy Wynn

The Rooms: Hildi adds sophistication to a living room by painting the walls slate gray, making butter yellow slipcovers, adding a touch of charcoal wax to an existing coffee table and side tables, and replacing the drop ceiling tiles with wood-tone panels. Vern uses the principles of feng shui in a living room by painting the walls and ceiling yellow for wealth, designing a coffee table that holds bamboo stalks for health, attaching small framed mirrors to the ceiling above a candle chandelier, and building a custom fish tank stand for the homeowner's large aquarium.

Lucky Vern: Vern removes the existing slipcover on the couch and discovers that the original upholstery color is cranberry, which perfectly matches his design.

Navel Alert!: Paige exposes her belly button for the first time while attaching Vern's mirrors to the ceiling.

Notable: Paige is nearly attacked by bees during the key swap.

Hildi's Room: ☺ ☺ ☹
Vern's Room: ☺ ☺ ☹

Providence: Wallis Avenue 💣 👶 ⌁

Cast: Paige, Genevieve, Frank, Amy Wynn

The Rooms: Gen brings a touch of Tuscany to a bedroom by painting the walls sage green, painting the ceiling yellow, installing floor-to-ceiling shelves, hanging ivy above the headboard, and using light and airy curtains and bed linens. Frank enlivens a kitchen by using several pastel shades of paint, creating a larger tabletop, laying a vinyl floor, and adding painted chevrons to the cabinets.

Notable: Frank uses his budget sparingly in order to buy the homeowners a dishwasher (they don't have one, and they have two kids). When Amy Wynn tells him that she can return two pieces of wood and enable him to buy the appliance, he does a touchdown victory dance.

Quotable Quote: Frank predicts the homeowners' reaction to the new dishwasher: "The squealing is gonna be like the Chicago stockyards when they see this."

Gen's Room: ☺ ☺ ☹
Frank's Room: ☺ ☺ ☹

Boston: Ashfield Street ♥

Cast: Paige, Laurie, Genevieve, Ty

The Rooms: Laurie breathes new life into a kids' room by painting the walls lavender, creating a trundle bed, painting the existing furniture white, and using ribbons as accents. Gen adds a Moroccan touch to a kid's room by painting the walls and ceiling deep blue, installing a large curtained bed, hanging a Moroccan metal lamp, using gold fabric accents, and hanging white draperies.

Oops!: Paige drills through a plastic place mat to create a lampshade, but the bit comes out of the drill. When Gen tries to pull the bit out of the place mat, she finds that they've drilled through the homeowners' deck. A huge giggle fit ensues.

Happy Ending: The girls who live in Laurie's room like her design so much that they actually turn cartwheels.

Laurie's Room: ☺ 😐 ☹
Gen's Room: ☺ 😐 ☹

Springfield: Sunset Terrace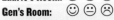

Cast: Paige, Hildi, Vern, Ty

The Rooms: Hildi creates a Victorian look in a living room by painting the walls light putty, using blue and white print fabric for draperies and slipcovers, painting blue stripes on the wood floor, sewing a white faux-fur rug, and transforming the fireplace with a custom-built Victorian-style mantelpiece. Vern goes for an even more Victorian look in the other living room by painting the walls yellow, highlighting the homeowners' French provincial furniture, laying a Victorian rug, making a light fixture with silver mesh and hand-strung beads, and creating a custom art piece using celestial and fleur-de-lis stencils.

Notable: Hildi and Vern design against type in this episode, with mixed results.

Hildi's Room: ☺ 😐 ☹
Vern's Room: ☺ 😐 ☹

Boston: Institute Road

Cast: Paige, Doug, Frank, Ty

The Rooms: Doug looks to the leaves for inspiration in his "Autumnal Bliss" bedroom. He papers the walls with bark paper, upholsters the headboard in linen, hangs yellow linen draperies, and frames fall leaves as art. Frank creates a Shakespearean library by painting the walls red, hand-painting Elizabethan musician cutouts for the walls, and painting a rounded stone pattern on the floor.

Quotable Quote: Frank, on what may be under the carpet he's ripping up: "It could be the gates of heaven or the portals of hell."

Notable: Ty skeletons down the driveway on a wheeled ottoman multiple times, nearly crashing into piles of lumber.

Doug's Room: ☺ 😐 ☹
Frank's Room: ☺ 😐 ☹

Philadelphia: Jeannes Street

Cast: Paige, Genevieve, Vern, Amy Wynn

The Rooms: Gen turns a basement den into a 3-D *Scrabble* board by painting taupe and white grids on the floors and ceiling, installing a black wall-length bar, making pillows that mimic *Scrabble* board squares, and framing game boards to hang on the wall. Vern uses the holiday season for inspiration in a living room by painting the walls and ceiling deep red, making camel slipcovers and draperies, and building a dark wood armoire with mirrored doors.

Silly Gen!: Gen and Paige try to screw lazy Susan tops to bar stools. First, Gen's screws aren't long enough; then they can't get the screws in, and Gen realizes she has the drill in reverse; next their screws are too long, and the tops won't swivel. A huge giggle fit breaks out.

Time Test: Vern's male homeowner takes forever to wrap

---

lights around two mini pine trees.

Gen's Room: ☺ 😐 ☹
Vern's Room: ☺ 😐 ☹

New Jersey: Perth Road

Cast: Paige, Frank, Laurie, Amy Wynn

The Rooms: Frank gives a living room a homier feel by adding light camel paint, a coffee table topped with a picture frame, textured folk art on the wall, and a custom-built armoire ("It's kind of a puppet theater cathedral"). Laurie redoes a bedroom without altering the existing Queen Anne furniture. She paints the walls a warm apricot, builds a custom canopy that rests on top of the four-poster bed, and adds bookshelves as nightstands.

Say What?: Frank describes his design as a "formal, casual, yet funky over-the-top look."

Boys Club: Frank's male homeowner complains about having to sew, because he doesn't think it's a manly activity. However, he also points out that he's secure in his manhood. Frank retorts, "Well, then if you're so damned secure, start putting that stuffing in that pillow."

Quotable Quote: While cutting tree branches to use in his room, Frank says, "I have a college degree. Reduced to a beaver."

Fashion Report: Laurie straightens her hair for this episode.

Frank's Room: ☺ 😐 ☹
Laurie's Room: ☺ 😐 ☹

Maryland: Village Green

Cast: Paige, Genevieve, Doug, Amy Wynn

The Rooms: Gen refines a bedroom by painting one wall chocolate brown, covering the ceiling with gold metallic paint, installing a custom geometric shelving unit, making a fountain, decoupaging sewing patterns to a wall, and creating a light fixture out of a large wicker ball. Doug creates an elegant and sophisticated look in a bedroom by painting the walls gray, building a large upholstered headboard with storage in the back, painting the furniture white, and painting large Matisse-inspired figures directly on the wall.

Oops!: To create custom lampshades, Gen wraps rounded glass vases with plastic wrap and then winds glued string around them à la papier-mâché. Once the vases are dry, Gen and Paige put on safety glasses and start hammering the shades to break the vases on the inside. Gen thinks her idea of including the plastic wrap will keep them from having to touch any shards of glass. She's wrong. After a huge giggle fit, Gen looks into the camera and warns, "This project isn't for kids."

Name Game: Doug titles his room "Strip Stripe" for the gray and white striped fabric he uses to cover the headboard.

Gen's Room: ☺ 😐 ☹
Doug's Room: ☺ 😐 ☹

Maryland: Fairway Court

Cast: Paige, Vern, Doug, Amy Wynn

The Rooms: Vern softens a bedroom by painting the walls a soft gray, hanging charcoal draperies, suspending a canopy over the existing sleigh bed, and dangling 100 clear crystals from the canopy edge. Doug designs a fantasy bedroom suite for train enthusiasts by rounding the ceiling edges, covering the walls with blue paint and fabric, and building fake walls and windows to mimic the inside of a Pullman car.

Quotable Quote: Vern states during Designer Chat, "Precision doesn't have to go overtime; you just have to be well-planned."

Notable: Doug claims that this design is the biggest challenge he's taken on in a *Trading Spaces* episode. Paige refers to it as a "marvelous achievement."

Vern's Room: ☺ 😐 ☹
Doug's Room: ☺ 😐 ☹

Chicago: Edward Road

Cast: Paige, Frank, Laurie, Ty

The Rooms: Frank adds patina to a kitchen by using touches of terra-cotta, copper, and green paint. He also lays earth-tone vinyl flooring, paints a faux-tile backsplash, makes a large floorcloth, and adds a butcher-block island. Laurie gives a living room a touch of European flair by painting a faux-fresco finish in yellow tones, installing dark wooden beams on the ceiling, hanging burlap draperies, painting a faux-inlay top on an occasional table, and repeating an X motif throughout the room.

Quotable Quote: At the end of Day 1 Frank says, "I'm gonna go home, have a pedicure, manicure, shower, have my designer stylist come in and...I'll see you in the morning."

Laurie's Design Theory: "I want to give them a room that is a basic skeleton with beautiful walls...and then, hopefully, what I trigger them to do is get a new love seat."

Frank's Room: ☺ 😐 ☹
Laurie's Room: ☺ 😐 ☹

Chicago: Spaulding Avenue 😮

Cast: Paige, Doug, Hildi, Ty

The Rooms: Doug adds a little funk to a living room by painting the walls yellow, using Venetian plaster to make black and yellow blocks on a wall, upholstering the furniture with zebra-print fabric, and suspending a tabletop from the ceiling to create a dining area. Hildi brings the outdoors into a bedroom. She paints the walls cream and the trim deep plum and then draws large "swooshes" of grass on the walls with pastels. She adds a row of grass planter boxes along one wall, uses bursts of orange in pillows, and installs a large wooden bed.

Conflict: Doug wants to glaze a 2-inch border around the wood floor. He paints a small strip to show what it will look like, and the homeowners argue against it. He wipes it off with a pouty face.

Sticky Situation: After drawing grass blades on the wall, Hildi and her homeowners seal the chalk pastel with several cans of hair spray.

Oops!: Ty can't get the window bench into the bedroom. He eventually has to remove the center legs to get it inside the bedroom door.

Doug's Room: ☺ 😐 ☹
Hildi's Room: ☺ 😐 ☹

163

Chicago: Fairview Avenue

Cast: Paige, Vern, Genevieve, Ty

The Rooms: Vern brightens a kitchen by painting the walls pear green, painting the cabinets white, creating a new cabinet for storage, making a new table, laying a black and white geometric rug, upholstering a storage bench that doubles as seating at the table, and hanging upholstered cushions against the wall above the bench. Gen gives the lodge look to a basement living room by painting the walls cinnamon, installing a pine plank ceiling, hanging wood wainscoting, slipcovering the furniture, and highlighting the fireplace with built-in shelves.

Oops!: Gen breaks the heel of her boot and goes to Ty for the repair.

Rest Time: Ty tries to take a break on a school bus, and Gen has to drag him back to work.

Vern's Room: ☺ 😐 ☹
Gen's Room: ☺ 😐 ☹

Colorado: Berry Avenue ❓ ☹

Cast: Paige, Genevieve, Hildi, Amy Wynn

The Rooms: Gen paints the walls of a kitchen bright eggplant, paints the cabinets vanilla-sage, removes the center panels of the cabinet doors to showcase the dishes inside, and prints each family member's face on a chair cover for personalized seating. Hildi creates an intimate living room by painting the walls a deep chocolate brown, using sage fabrics, transforming the coffee table into a large ottoman, and installing a wall-size fountain made to mimic the existing windows.

Yucky Moment: Gen explains her color choices by tearing apart a boiled artichoke. Paige pops the bitter heart into her mouth and nearly gags.

Resourceful: Gen sketches her table design—including measurements—on Amy Wynn's palm.

Joke Time: Gen's homeowners rent a jackhammer and use it in a bucket of hardened concrete to make their neighbors think their floor is being ripped out.

Technical Stuff: Gen attempts to explain how she uses her laptop to reproduce the family photos for the chair covers. Gen describes the computer program she's using as a "special program for a special girl."

Silly Stuff: During Designer Chat, Paige and Gen wear the chair covers with the homeowners' faces over their heads and role-play the homeowners' reaction to their new room.

What Was She Thinking?: Hildi and Paige cover the bottom of a plastic window box planter with silicone to seal it. When they try to set a large piece of glass in the box to create the fountain, Paige cuts through the silicone, breaking the seal. Water quickly seeps across the wood floor.

Gen's Room: ☺ 😐 ☹
Hildi's Room: ☺ 😐 ☹

Colorado: Cherry Street

Cast: Paige, Genevieve, Laurie, Amy Wynn

The Rooms: Gen gives a living room a punch of personality by painting the walls brick red with sage accents, hanging antlers on the walls, installing floor-to-ceiling shelving, making a focal point out of one of the homeowners' landscape photos, and creating an inlaid rug. Laurie applies a touch of mod to a living room by painting gray and yellow horizontal stripes on the walls, building a new glass-top coffee table, hanging silver silk draperies, and adding a piece of custom artwork.

Quotable Quote: Gen describes the original look of her room by saying, "If this were a country, it would be Beigeland."

What Was She Thinking?: Rather than lay a green rug on top of the beige carpet, Gen cuts out a patch of the carpet and lays the new rug inside. Gen warns viewers, "Don't do this if you're renting."

Gen's Room: ☺ 😐 ☹
Laurie's Room: ☺ 😐 ☹

Colorado: Andes Way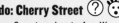

Cast: Paige, Frank, Vern, Amy Wynn

The Rooms: Frank creates a family-friendly living room by rag-rolling the walls with cream and peach paint, hanging valances coated with brown builder's paper, building a white and sage armoire, and creating a kids' nook with a large art table, plant murals on the walls, and wooden clouds nailed to the ceiling. Vern stripes a living room, laying two colors of laminate flooring in alternating stripes, painting a red horizontal stripe on the khaki walls, and continuing the same stripe across the draperies.

Say What?: Describing his paint technique, Frank says, "It's kinda, like, goth-eyed wonky."

Notable: When Amy Wynn gives up on helping out with one of Frank's crafts project, he calls her a "craft wimp."

Frank's Room: ☺ 😐 ☹
Vern's Room: ☺ 😐 ☹

Colorado: Stoneflower Drive

Cast: Paige, Frank, Doug, Amy Wynn

The Rooms: Frank injects some whimsy into a bedroom by painting the walls celadon green, building a large headboard that mimics a skyline, creating a matching dog bed, and hanging gold curtains. Doug updates a living room with a design he calls "Smoke Screen." He paints the walls moss green, adds pewter accents, hangs pleated metal screening, and builds screen doors to cover fireplace shelving.

Gotcha!: Frank brings in tacky dolphin pillows, and the homeowner says that she loves them. Frank laughs and explains that he's only using them as inexpensive pillow forms.

Helping Out: Doug lounges in a deck chair drinking iced tea while reading faux-finish directions to his homeowners. He tosses them supplies instead of getting up.

Wise Words: Frank, during Designer Chat: "I wanted to give them a room that has, like most relationships or marriages, some whimsy, some peacefulness, and a little bit of tactile sensitivity and sexuality."

Frank's Room: ☺ 😐 ☹
Doug's Room: ☺ 😐 ☹

Seattle: 137th Street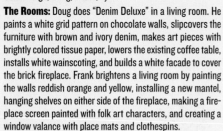

Cast: Paige, Doug, Frank, Ty

The Rooms: Doug does "Denim Deluxe" in a living room. He paints a white grid pattern on chocolate walls, slipcovers the furniture with brown and ivory denim, makes art pieces with brightly colored tissue paper, lowers the existing coffee table, installs white wainscoting, and builds a white facade to cover the brick fireplace. Frank brightens a living room by painting the walls reddish orange and yellow, installing a new mantel, hanging shelves on either side of the fireplace, making a fireplace screen painted with folk art characters, and creating a window valance with place mats and clothespins.

Conflict: Homeowner dissension abounds in this classic episode! The living room homeowners leave Doug strict instructions not to paint their fireplace, but of course, Doug wants to paint it white. His homeowners repeatedly argue with him about it. When Doug states that he's not happy, one of his homeowners turns ultrapositive and says, "It's OK not to be happy sometimes!" When Doug leaves the room in a huff, she looks to the camera and says, "Well, now he's a little cranky."

Resourceful?: While Doug pouts, Ty problem-solves by designing a facade to "slipcover" the brick. As he and Ty are installing the facade, Doug prophetically says, "This may be my shining moment."

Nasty Side: While working with Paige and his homeowners to make the tissue paper art, Doug places a wooden Santa figure on the table and says that he brought Frank along to oversee their crafting.

Huh?: Frank describes what he wants to paint on the walls by saying, "We're going to be doing a kind of rectangular, kind of checky, not really country, not really contemporary, just homey, cottagey, but with a kind of a more upbeat level."

Reveal-ing Moments: A classic Reveal that must be seen to be believed! The denim living room homeowners are extremely disappointed with their room (the male homeowner surmises Doug's design as "I see a lot of firewood"), and the female homeowner leaves the room in tears while her microphone continues running.

Doug's Room: ☺ 😐 ☹
Frank's Room: ☺ 😐 ☹

Seattle: Dakota Street

Cast: Paige, Vern, Laurie, Ty

The Rooms: Vern adds drama and romance to a living room by painting the walls golden yellow, hanging brown draperies, building an armoire with red upholstered door panels, slipcovering the furniture in white fabric dyed with

---

tea bags, and constructing red candle torchères. Laurie tries to convince her homeowners that she can warm up a bedroom with parchment-color paint, soft white and blue fabrics, various chocolate brown accents on the furniture and headboard, and painted partition screens.

Guy Thing: Vern's male homeowner sits down at the sewing machine and is confused about how to make it "go."

Yucky Moment: Paige catches a large fish while standing in a fish market during the introduction.

Reveal-ing Moment: Both of the female homeowners dislike their rooms. In fact, the bedroom homeowner hates her room and keeps talking about all the work she'll have to do the next day to change it.

Vern's Room: ☺ 😐 ☹
Laurie's Room: ☺ 😐 ☹

Seattle: 56th Place ☹

Cast: Paige, Hildi, Genevieve, Ty

The Rooms: Hildi covers a basement rec room in magenta and taupe fabric hung from the ceiling. She also builds new coffee and side tables and slipcovers new sofas with magenta fabric. Gen creates an Asian living room, using shimmery silver and red paints and coating one wall in a metal paint that oxidizes to a rusted finish. She makes a valance out of an obi and uses cedar flowerpots as picture frames.

Oops!: While Gen and Paige are crafting a lamp, they recount all of the bad things that have happened when they work on projects together. While lamenting all the things they've broken, Paige slips with the glass globe she's cleaning and breaks it. Gen states, "This is a show of human errors."

Notable: Hildi surprises her homeowners by spray-painting the existing upholstered furniture magenta. Later, one of Hildi's homeowners brings Paige in with her eyes closed and then reveals the painted furniture. Paige is shocked and says that it looks bad.

Budget Crisis: Hildi arrives on Day 2 to find that the tarp blew off the freshly painted furniture; the furniture has been rained on and ruined. Paige eventually agrees to break the rules, letting Hildi go severely over budget in order to buy new furniture. Hildi leaves, and returns with two new sofas (total cost: $500) that are eventually slipcovered.

Hildi's Room: ☺ 😐 ☹
Gen's Room: ☺ 😐 ☹

Oregon: Alyssum Avenue

Cast: Paige, Hildi, Genevieve, Amy Wynn

The Rooms: Hildi cozies a bedroom by upholstering the walls and ceiling with silver-blue fabric, building a bed from storage cubes, draping sheer white fabric from the ceiling center over the bed corners, hanging a chandelier above the bed, and adding a blue monogram to white bed linens. Gen adds a graphic touch to a living room by painting the walls bright yellow, covering a wall with 6-inch squares, building cedar shelving under the stairs, and hanging clotheslines to display art and photos.

Never-Ending Project: Gen's wall of squares requires a ridiculous number of steps. The design calls for more than a thousand squares of wood; each square has to be stacked on top of others to create different heights; and the stacked squares must be glued together, stapled to reinforce the glue, primed, painted, hung on the wall, and puttied over to cover the nail holes.

Hildi's Room: ☺ 😐 ☹
Gen's Room: ☺ 😐 ☹

Oregon: Alsea Court

Cast: Paige, Frank, Laurie, Amy Wynn

The Rooms: Frank goes south of the border in a kitchen by painting a serape on the ceiling, making a basket-weave wall treatment with sheet metal strips, painting the cabinet door center panels silver, designing a distressed tabletop, and upholstering dining chairs with serape fabric. Laurie brings warmth to a living room by painting the walls amber, using several expensive fabrics in warm harvest shades, building a long armoire with gold filigree door insets, and designing a large central ottoman.

Quotable Quotes: Frank again: "I feel very Carmen Miranda-ish. Now, quick, get me a pineapple drink and a funny hat."

Frank's Room: ☺ 😐 ☹
Laurie's Room: ☺ 😐 ☹

Portland: Everett Street

Cast: Paige, Doug, Vern, Amy Wynn

The Rooms: Doug transforms a family room into an Art Deco theater by painting the floors and ceiling chocolate brown, covering the walls with chocolate brown fabric, building graduated platforms for silver chairs, suspending the television from the ceiling, and installing aisle lights. Vern creates a cohesive look in a living/dining room by painting the walls sage green and hanging sage draperies with white satin stripes on the windows and the walls of the dining area. He also builds a custom armoire and buffet with square wooden insets stained various colors and creates a custom lampshade with handmade art paper.

Fashion Report: Doug wears a knit skullcap; Vern's hair is especially spiky.

Conflict: Doug's homeowners continually question whether there will be room for a computer in the finished design. By the morning of Day 2, Doug is weary of fending them off and mixes a glass of antacid.

Guy Thing: Vern explains stuffing a pillow and mounting a wall sconce to his male homeowner by relating these processes to taxidermy, the homeowner's hobby.

Doug's Room: ☺ 😐 ☹
Vern's Room: ☺ 😐 ☹

Santa Clara: Lafayette Street

Cast: Paige, Frank, Laurie, Ty

The Rooms: Frank adds a festive touch to the living room of a Delta Gamma residence by painting the walls two shades of a peachy orange; highlighting the curved ceiling with stenciled stars, triangles, swirls, and dots; painting the sorority letters above the fireplace; and installing a window bench seat. Laurie updates the Delta Gamma chapter room by painting the walls a muted seafoam, stenciling yellow anchors on the walls, designing a coffee table with hidden additional seating, and making a candelabra out of a captain's wheel.

Paint Fun: Frank reveals the wall colors by having both the sorority sisters close their eyes, dip their hands in the paint, and then smear it on the walls.

Notable: Frank does a cartwheel during the sped-up footage of his team removing furniture from his room.

Go, Girl: Laurie reminisces about her sorority days as a Kappa and talks about having to dress up like Carmen Miranda and sing "Kappa, Kappa-cabana" to the tune of Barry Manilow's "Copacabana."

Acting!: Paige pretends to be a surprised sorority sister at the last Reveal and starts screaming and hugging the sorority members.

Budget Crunch: Over budget by II cents, Laurie presents Paige with that amount during Designer Chat.

Frank's Room: ☺ 😐 ☹
Laurie's Room: ☺ 😐 ☹

California: Corte Rosa ☹

Cast: Paige, Vern, Laurie, Ty

The Rooms: Vern gives a bedroom an exotic resort decor by painting the walls light chino, upholstering the bedside tabletops with faux leather, adding tribal- and safari-print

---

fabrics to the draperies and bed linens, hanging a red glass light fixture, and building storage cabinets on a large plant ledge. Laurie creates romance in a bedroom by painting the walls sage green, hanging a French tester canopy above the bed, painting the existing furniture mocha brown, installing a window seat with storage cabinets, and hanging dark green draperies.

For Fun: Vern, Laurie, and Ty pedal tiny three-wheeled bikes at the start of the show.

Quotable Quote: Commenting on the romance of his room, Vern says to Paige during his Designer Chat, "If this doesn't produce a third child, this is gonna be a total failure."

Vern's Room: ☺ 😐 ☹
Laurie's Room: ☺ 😐 ☹

California: Grenadine Way

Cast: Paige, Vern, Frank, Ty

The Rooms: Vern looks to vintage Indian fabrics for inspiration in a bedroom. He paints the walls soft blue, lays wood laminate flooring, installs a large headboard of basket-woven iridescent fabric, and hangs amber glass candleholders. Frank gives ethnic flair to a living room by painting a mantel with lines of mustard, white, taupe, and black, designing a large wooden sculpture, and building a new coffee table, armoire, and valance.

Get Well!: Vern has laryngitis this episode and is often barely able to speak. He tells Ty on Day I that he's doing his best Darth Vader impersonation. By the morning of Day 2, he has to communicate with his homeowners by writing on pieces of paper.

Quotable Quote: Frank describes for Paige how he feels about staying under budget, saying simply, "I'm puffed."

Notable: Penny-wise Vern is over budget (!) by $2.47.

Vern's Room: ☺ 😐 ☹
Frank's Room: ☺ 😐 ☹

Berkeley: Prospect Street

Cast: Paige, Doug, Genevieve, Ty

The Rooms: Doug cleans up the Delta Upsilon fraternity chapter room (and goes "DU-clectic") by painting the walls lime green, installing bench seating, constructing two huge circular ottomans upholstered with lime and orange fabrics, and suspending a tabletop from the ceiling. Gen adds classic Hollywood-style glamour to the Alpha Omicron Pi sorority chapter room by painting white and silver stripes on the walls, adding black and silver throw pillows, building a large armoire, and commissioning her team to trace silhouettes of Paige and herself for wall art.

Fashion Report: Doug dons leather pants (and a crisp blue oxford shirt, of course). Paige sports black, horn-rimmed glasses at the start of the show.

Yucky Moments: Doug is amazed by how filthy his assigned room is. When it's time to clear the room, Doug starts pitching everything out the third-story window—including the sofa. Later, he has his team put on biohazard gear to sweep and clean the room before they start redecorating.

Huh?: Gen tells her eager team members that she wants to create "a couch that screams 'Sexy, sexy, sexy!'"

Diva Fit Details: When Doug points out that one of his team members missed a spot while painting, she paints his shirt. A full-fledged paint fight ensues.

Conflict: Doug's team fights to keep the existing beer lights in the room, rejecting the custom lights Doug wants to make. Doug eventually gives in.

Doug's Room: ☺ 😐 ☹
Gen's Room: ☺ 😐 ☹

Oakland: Webster Street

Cast: Paige, Hildi, Genevieve, Amy Wynn

The Rooms: Hildi experiments in a living room by covering the walls with straw. She also installs a wall of bookshelves, covers the fireplace with copper mesh and glass rods, and screens the windows with wooden louvered blinds. Gen brightens a kitchen by painting the cabinets yellow and the walls cobalt blue, building a tile-top island and kids' table, personalizing dishware with family art and photos, and designing a backlit display shelf for a glass bottle collection.

The Last Straw: Hildi's wall treatment turns out to be high-maintenance. She and her homeowners spend much time brushing off straw that didn't adhere and hand-trimming long pieces.

Quotable Quote: Hildi is truly amazed when one of her homeowners explains that the kids who will live in the room may tear straw off the walls and eat it. Hildi questions the homeowner's concern by asking, "Do they eat lint off of the sofa?" The homeowner tells her the children do. Hildi then asks, "Do they walk around outside and eat grass?" The homeowner tells her they do indeed.

Fashion Report: Gen has her hair wrapped in numerous tight little buns à la Scary Spice. One of her homeowners uses a hair bun as a pincushion while sewing. Gen lets her hair down for her Designer Chat, to voluminous effect.

Reveal-ing Moments: The living room homeowners seem to like the design but are unsure about having straw on the walls with two young children in the household. When they demonstrate how the kids will pick at the straw, Paige eats two small pieces of straw.

Hildi's Room: ☺ 😐 ☹
Gen's Room: ☺ 😐 ☹

California: Peralta Street

Cast: Paige, Hildi, Doug, Amy Wynn

The Rooms: Hildi divides a living room into quadrants by painting two opposite corners of the room and ceiling silver and painting the remaining corners and ceiling space violet. She supplements the look with a clear-glass mosaic on the fireplace surround, four metal chairs, and a large circular ottoman upholstered in silver and violet. Doug thinks pink in a dining room. He paints the walls bubble gum pink, paints the ceiling chocolate brown, upholsters new dining chairs with lime green T-shirts, and tops new storage units with green gazing balls.

Musical Moments: In this tuneful episode, the four homeowners play together in their band as Doug and Hildi dance at the start of the show. Later, Doug attempts to rap, and Hildi plays guitar badly while assigning homework to her team.

Oops!: Hildi attempts to drill through four large stones so she can attach them as legs on her ottoman. That doesn't work, so she has to use an adhesive to connect them.

Yucky Moment: Hildi photocopies parts of her own body to make wall art.

Nasty Side: Doug throws all the homeowners' knickknacks into the trash at the start of the show.

Hildi's Room: ☺ 😐 ☹
Doug's Room: ☺ 😐 ☹

Los Angeles: Willoughby Avenue ☹

Cast: Paige, Doug, Genevieve, Ty

The Rooms: Doug sees red in a living room: He stencils the walls and doors in red and white, using a rectangular graphic based on a pillow pattern. He paints the ceiling gray, lays a red shag rug, and builds a U-shape couch with red upholstery. Gen designs a swingin' living room with 1950s flair by painting the walls aqua, covering floor stains with black paint, transforming mod place mats into wall sconces, slipcovering a futon in white vinyl, and laying a bookcase on its side to create a new coffee table.

Fashion Report: Gen wears a Britney Spears-inspired tube sock on her arm. Doug's leather pants make another appearance, and he appears to be growing a goatee.

Safety First!: When Paige and Gen go to a local flower market to buy orchids late on Day 2, Gen runs across the street without looking both ways.

Flaming Success: Gen lights a cigar with a blowtorch when her room comes together.

Gen's Design Theory: "I think it's important whenever you do something that's remotely hip...that you are able to update. Otherwise you're stuck in something that becomes very passé."

Reveal-ing Moments: Both male homeowners swear during The Reveals and have to be bleeped.

Quotable Quote: During the end credits, Doug's male homeowner does a fine Paige impression, saying, "Hi, America. I'm Paige Davis. Look at my cute little Sandy Duncan hair."

Doug's Room: ☺ 😐 ☹
Gen's Room: ☺ 😐 ☹

Los Angeles: Springdale Drive

Cast: Paige, Vern, Laurie, Ty

The Rooms: Vern brightens a dining room by painting the walls yellow, hanging bronze draperies, installing a wall-length buffet with built-in storage, and designing a multi-armed halogen chandelier with gold vellum shades and a hanging candleholder. Laurie enlivens a basement den by painting the walls yellow, slipcovering the existing furniture with natural cotton duck fabric, sewing an aqua Roman shade, installing several yellow and aqua shadow box shelves, designing a folding screen to mask exercise equipment, and painting squares and rectangles in various shades of aqua to create custom wall art.

Oops!: Vern's homeowners write positive thoughts on the walls in pencil, with the intent of painting over them as they work on the room. The writing shows through the paint, and they have to go back and clean off what they wrote.

Guy Thing: Vern and Ty have trouble bringing in the buffet. It's too long to make several of the turns in the house, and they bump the corner of it on a doorway, scuffing the piece.

Vern's Room: ☺ 😐 ☹
Laurie's Room: ☺ 😐 ☹

California: Abbeywood Lane

Cast: Paige, Frank, Hildi, Ty

The Rooms: Frank gives a living room a cohesive look by painting the walls sage green; building an upholstered wall hanging in shades of peach, coral, and yellow; painting a life-size image of the homeowners' toddler on the wall; making throw pillows out of fabric designed by the homeowner; and crafting candleholders out of 4×4s covered with license plates. Hildi creates her version of a nautical living room by painting the walls black; nailing lightly stained 1×2s on the walls in a vertical arrangement; building two large couches; using seafoam fabric to upholster the couch, create throw pillows, and make draperies; and mounting photos of the ocean onto blocks of wood.

Oops!: Ty demolishes the existing pass-through in Frank's room and takes a chunk of the wall with it.

Notable: Paige and Frank "kiss" while wearing dust masks.

Frank's Room: ☺ 😐 ☹
Hildi's Room: ☺ 😐 ☹

Austin: La Costa Drive (celebrity episode)

Cast: Paige, Vern, Hildi, Ty

The Rooms: In the first celebrity episode of *Trading*

Spaces, Vern breathes life into the bonus room of Dixie Chicks lead vocalist Natalie Maines. Vern paints the walls yellow, installs a wall-length desk and sewing unit, hangs a huge chandelier, and sews throw pillows, draperies, and bed linens with shimmery red fabric. Hildi adds style to a sewing room, which belongs to Natalie's mother, by rail-roading gray and sage fabric on the walls, installing wooden louvered wall dividers, building a 14-foot couch, reupholstering a vintage shampoo chair, and covering a coffee table with slate tiles.

Call-In: Ty is too busy to come over to Vern's room during Day 1, so Vern phones in his measurements to him.

Quick Chick: Hildi and Natalie have a sewing race while working on the couch bolsters. Natalie wins.

Vern's Room: ☺ 😐 ☹
Hildi's Room: ☺ 😐 ☹

Texas: Sherwood Street

Cast: Paige, Frank, Genevieve, Amy Wynn

The Rooms: Frank transforms a kitchen by removing strawberry wallpaper, sponge-painting a focal point wall, hanging new draperies with a pear motif, painting the avocado green floor and countertops with faux tiles, and hanging a thin plywood sunburst around the existing fluorescent light. Gen conjures a New England cottage feel in a bedroom by painting three of the walls pale smoke, painting one of the walls ultrabright white, building a fireplace mantel-style headboard, creating curtain tiebacks from red neckties, sewing bed pillows from pinstriped suit jackets, distressing the existing ceiling fan, and adding a library nook.

Quotable Quote: Frank calms his homeowners' fears of a new painting technique by saying, "I will take you by the hand, lead you to the river of paint, dip you in it, and baptize you to the great religion of faux finishes."

Resourceful: Near the end of Day 2, Gen pulls in a stone bench from the garden because she can't afford to buy one.

Reveal-ing Moments: The kitchen homeowners love their room so much they won't stop screeching. Paige eventually puts her fingers in her ears.

Frank's Room: ☺ 😐 ☹
Gen's Room: ☺ 😐 ☹

Houston: Sawdust Street

? ✳ $ ♥

Cast: Paige, Laurie, Doug, Amy Wynn

The Rooms: Laurie refines a living room by painting the walls margarine yellow, building a wall-length bookshelf, hanging bamboo blinds and yellow drapery panels, and adding two spicy orange chairs. Doug goes "Zen/Goth" in a living room by painting the walls blood red, building an L-shape couch, hanging a large wrought-iron light fixture, and blowing up a photo of the female homeowner in lingerie and knee-high boots to hang over the fireplace.

Notable: Laurie announces that she is pregnant.

Oops!: Laurie's homeowners do such a bad job painting the bookshelf that Laurie has them scrape off the paint and redo it.

Sketchy: Doug draws his couch design for Amy Wynn on toy magnetic drawing board.

Resourceful: Doug steals a pool noodle (to stuff his couch's bolster) from a kid playing in a pool. The kid chases after him, yelling, "Give me back my noodle!"

Yucky Moment: Doug finds the revealing photo to hang over the fireplace by digging through the female homeowner's drawers.

Laurie's Room: ☺ 😐 ☹
Doug's Room: ☺ 😐 ☹

Houston: Appalachian Trail  ✳

Cast: Paige, Doug, Laurie, Amy Wynn

The Rooms: Laurie adds style to an office/playroom by painting the walls terra-cotta, building a large shelving and desk unit with plumbing conduit, painting the existing coffee table and armoire in eggshell and black, adding new seating, and creating the illusion of symmetry with cream draperies on an off-center window. Doug goes for a soft look in a bedroom by painting the walls pale blue, upholstering a tall headboard in blue chenille, sewing new blue and white bed linens, and installing custom light fixtures.

Fashion Report: Doug appears to suddenly have a fair amount of gray hair.

Name Game: Doug titles his room "A Pretty Room *by Doug*" (and yes, the italics are important).

Cheer Up!: Doug's female homeowner is a cheerleading coach. Her squad appears in the driveway and does a cheer for Doug: "Fix that space. You're an ace. Go, Doug, Go. You're a pro." Perhaps inspired by the cheerleading, Doug does a cartwheel later in the show.

Doug's Room: ☺ 😐 ☹
Laurie's Room: ☺ 😐 ☹

Plano: Bent Horn Court ☹

Cast: Paige, Genevieve, Vern, Ty

The Rooms: Gen regresses as she designs a playroom, painting multicolor polka dots on the walls, cutting movable circles of outdoor carpeting for the floors, building a large castle-shape puppet theater, hanging fabric-covered tire swings, and designing four upholstered squares on wheels, with storage space inside. Vern gets in touch with his rustic side in a living room by laying natural-color adhesive carpet tiles, painting an existing armoire and other furniture pieces black, and building a combination ottoman/coffee table/bench unit.

Go, Girl: Gen sends Paige on a mission around the house to find objects with different textures that Gen can frame and hang as kid-friendly art.

Gen's Room: ☺ 😐 ☹
Vern's Room: ☺ 😐 ☹

Plano: Shady Valley Road 👶

Cast: Paige, Hildi, Doug, Ty

The Rooms: Hildi creates a two-tone bedroom by painting the walls bright white, installing 12-inch orange baseboards, building a new head- and footboard that match the pitch of the cathedral ceiling and covering them with white slipcovers, and upholstering a chair with white faux fur. Doug adds sophisticated style to a playroom by painting the wall moss green ("Moss Madness"), installing beams on the ceiling in a barnlike formation, building a basket-weave armoire, revamping a futon into a daybed, and hanging bifold doors on a toy closet.

Gifted: The two female homeowners are budding interior designers and have a business making accessories. They present Paige with a small lamp during the key swap.

Conflict: Hildi plans to dye the carpet in her room orange, but her female homeowner is adamantly opposed to the idea. They have several discussions about dyeing the carpet, with the homeowner becoming increasingly forceful in her opposition. At one point, Hildi asks rhetorically why she's been asked to design the room if she's not going to be allowed to follow through on her vision, noting, "Everyone in America knows I can rip up that carpet if I want to." Hildi compromises by sprinkling orange flower petals across the carpet for the Reveal.)

Hildi's Room: ☺ 😐 ☹
Doug's Room: ☺ 😐 ☹

Texas: Sutton Court $

Cast: Paige, Laurie, Frank, Ty

The Rooms: Laurie designs a kitchen, using the homeowners' china for inspiration. She paints the walls taupe with white trim, builds large wooden shadow boxes to display china pieces, hangs new light fixtures, and uses taupe fabric for the window treatments and chair cushions. Frank works with a Southwest theme in a living room, adding chamois-cloth accents to the existing furniture, building a footstool out of a saddle, hanging several custom-made art pieces, designing a Mission-style armoire, and making potted cactus out of vegetables.

Notable: Frank is hoarse throughout the episode and tells Paige, "I sound bad, but I am so perky."

Laurie's Room: ☺ 😐 ☹
Frank's Room: ☺ 😐 ☹

Raleigh: Legging Lane

Cast: Paige, Frank, Hildi, Amy Wynn

The Rooms: Hildi adds romance to a bedroom by painting the walls slate gray, hanging smoky plum draperies, sewing a tufted lavender coverlet, framing a favorite picture of the Eiffel Tower, and building cubic bench seats and nightstands. Frank lets his creativity flow in a playroom by painting walls, furniture, doors, and floors in a multitude of pastel colors. He also hides a large refrigerator, builds an armoire to house media equipment, and designs a large toy chest.

Oops!: When Paige brings the homeowners into Hildi's room for the Reveal, she accidentally leads the male homeowner into the TV stand, banging his leg.

Paint Explosion!: Frank uses paint in every shade of the rainbow—and then some.

Frank's Room: ☺ 😐 ☹
Hildi's Room: ☺ 😐 ☹

North Carolina: Southerby Drive ✳

Cast: Paige, Doug, Hildi, Amy Wynn

The Rooms: Doug adds an Eastern touch to a bedroom by painting the walls china blue and painting white chinoiserie murals. He builds a black four-poster bed with PVC pipe, adds a custom-built sculpture, hangs white draperies, and paints the furniture black. Hildi also displays Eastern influences in a bedroom, painting the walls a soft green and installing a wall of shoji screens to create a headboard. She covers the screens and the existing furniture with lavender crackle finish, hangs lavender draperies, and upholsters with purple fabric.

Quotable Quote: Hildi's female homeowner says to her while upholstering, "Why did I ever doubt you, Hildi?"

Doug's Room: ☺ 😐 ☹
Hildi's Room: ☺ 😐 ☹

Wake Forest: Rodney Bay ✳

Cast: Paige, Vern, Laurie, Amy Wynn

The Rooms: Vern adds drama to a bedroom by painting the walls gray, attaching a fabric canopy to the ceiling, designing a headboard with interior lights that shine out of the top, painting the existing furniture black, and upholstering a chair with gray flannel. Laurie brightens a living room by painting the walls a bold shade of green, installing two floor-to-ceiling shelving units with crown molding, hanging yellow draperies, adding several pillows in warm harvest shades to the existing off-white sofa, and hanging a new parchment-shade light fixture.

Quotable Quote: In order to convince her homeowners that she must remove the existing ceiling fan, Laurie states, "I cannot in good faith do this room and not do this."

Reveal-ing Moments: Both sets of homeowners love their rooms, but the male living room homeowner swears twice upon opening his eyes and finding that the ceiling fan is gone. He vows to hang it up by the next morning.

Vern's Room: ☺ 😐 ☹
Laurie's Room: ☺ 😐 ☹

Season 3

Maine: George Road ❓

Cast: Paige, Doug, Genevieve, Ty

The Rooms: Doug adds warmth to a kitchen by painting the walls umber, painting the woodwork white, installing a butcher-block countertop, building a large pantry unit with bifold doors, and sewing a large tablecloth. Gen updates a dark kitchen by painting the walls bright green, installing a black and white tile countertop, building a butcher-block island, hanging wood laminate wall paneling, and installing a 1930s light fixture.

Quotable Quotes: Doug's female homeowner tells her husband that Doug is "easy on the eyes." She goes on to say, "He hasn't been a real jerk yet."

Yucky Moments: Doug, Ty, and Paige make several laxative and lubricant jokes because the new countertop has to be rubbed with mineral oil.

Girl Power: When Gen's male homeowner gets a bit too excited about working with a pretty young woman, Gen takes control of the situation, telling him, "If I can handle power tools, I can handle you."

Budget Boasting: When Gen learns her budget is at $776.52, she looks into the camera and says, "Beat that, Doug!"

Doug's Room: ☺ 😐 ☹
Gen's Room: ☺ 😐 ☹

Portland: Rosemont Avenue ✳

Cast: Paige, Laurie, Vern, Ty

The Rooms: Laurie goes nautical in a living room by painting the walls deep aqua blue, painting the fireplace white, putting a cream-tone paint wash on wooden chairs and upholstering them with zebra-print fabric, and installing a vintage mercury glass chandelier. Vern brightens a living room by painting the walls yellow, hanging black and yellow Roman shades, installing French doors, covering the ceiling with white steel squares, hanging a ceiling fan, using black slipcovers for the existing furniture, and adding silver fold-up trays to serve as side tables and a coffee table.

Design Insight: Laurie says this is the first time that her paint color choice on *Trading Spaces* was not inspired by fabric. (Her inspiration in this case was the name of the paint color, which refers to the bay where the episode was filmed.)

Notable: Vern actually installs an all-white ceiling fan in his room! He points out that it's a *Trading Spaces* first.

Laurie's Room: ☺ 😐 ☹
Vern's Room: ☺ 😐 ☹

Maine: Joseph Drive ✳ 👶 ❓

Cast: Paige, Laurie, Frank, Ty

The Rooms: Laurie enlivens a bedroom by painting the walls soft yellow, building an Asian-style shelving unit, designing a new headboard, sewing gray and white toile bedding, and adding an unusual floral light fixture. Frank shows another side of his design style in a bachelor's bedroom. He paints the walls and ceiling dark blue-green, hangs simple white draperies, sews a large plastic envelope to hold a pencil drawing of a leaf on the wall, builds a table that houses three wooden bins, and jazzes up a rocking chair with pet collars.

Notable: This is Laurie's last show before having her baby.

Quotable Quote: Frank, on his room design: "I want this to be the pit of wild monkey love."

Really?: Frank repeatedly tells anyone who will listen that this room will not contain any faux finishes or distressed objects. When Paige challenges him and says that he'll paint a chicken somewhere, he claims that he's only painted a chicken once in the history of *Trading Spaces*.

Laugh Riot: Frank and one of his homeowners make custom candleholders with metal pipe nipples and flanges. The homeowner becomes giggly at the mention of pipe nipples, and she and Frank can't stop laughing throughout the project.

Yucky Moment: Frank straps pet collars on an existing rocking chair, explaining coyly that they can function as arm and leg restraints for visitors to the bachelor pad.

Laurie's Room: ☺ 😐 ☹
Frank's Room: ☺ 😐 ☹

Long Island: Steuben Boulevard

Cast: Paige, Edward, Frank, Ty

The Rooms: Edward jazzes up a bedroom by painting the walls light mocha, hanging wall sconces, building an Art Deco armoire, painting Deco patterns on the closet doors, installing lights around the bottom edge of the bed frame, hanging a canopy, and painting a faux-malachite finish on the furniture tops and wall sconces. Frank gets woodsy in a dining room, painting the walls deep orange, installing pine doors between the dining room and kitchen, creating a coffee table out of a large flowerpot, painting white birch trees all around the room, and making a large pig-topped weather vane to sit above the fireplace.

Notable: Edward makes his designer debut in this episode.
A Compliment?: Ty finishes installing the bed light, turns it on, and tells Edward, "It looks like Vegas!"
Getting Personal: Frank admits to a fear of heights.
Name Game: Frank names the weather vane pig "Poopalina."

Edward's Room: ☺ 😐 ☹
Frank's Room: ☺ 😐 ☹

Long Island: Split Rock Road ❓

Cast: Paige, Genevieve, Vern, Amy Wynn

The Rooms: Gen brightens a dark kitchen by painting the walls white, the trim celadon green, the window shutters pale blue, and the cabinets yellow. Gen also polishes the existing copper stove hood, hangs white wooden slats on one wall, builds a butcher-block table, skirts the dining chairs in white fabric, and coats a new light fixture with copper spray paint. Vern adds a soft touch to a kitchen by painting the walls and cabinet door insets green, painting parts of the cabinet doors white, stenciling white fleurs-de-lis on the cabinet doors, building a new laminate countertop, laying a two-tone parquet floor, using green toile fabrics on Roman shades and table linens, adding touches of green gingham to the tablecloth, and adding several green-shaded table lamps to the countertop.

Dance Break: Gen dances to shake a can of spray paint.

What Was She Thinking?: Wanting to make candleholders out of pieces of rock, Gen tries to drill into the rock with a carbide bit that she was assured could handle the job. (Didn't she remember the California: Peralta Street episode in which Hildi had similar problems?!) After several attempts, Gen looks into the camera and says, "I suggest buying candleholders at the local hardware store."

Notable: Gen's inspiration for her design is a necklace that the homeowner wears nearly every day.

Gen's Room: ☺ 😐 ☹
Vern's Room: ☺ 😐 ☹

New York: Whitlock Road 👶

Cast: Paige, Genevieve, Doug, Amy Wynn

The Rooms: Gen designs a bedroom with an espresso color scheme: She paints the walls café au lait, uses darker java on the ceiling beams, and paints sections of the ceiling cream. She also sews orange asterisks on a white bedspread, builds a combination headboard/desk, and exposes original

167

wood flooring. Doug updates a bedroom by painting squares on the wall in multiple shades of sage, building a mantel-like headboard, designing S-shape side tables, sewing stripes of yarn on a white bedspread, and framing strips of wood veneer for bedside art.

Fashion Report: Paige wears a tank top or, rather, several matching tank tops featuring phrases that relate to each scene of the show: Key Swap, Blue Team, Red Team, Gen, and Doug.

Yucky Moment: Gen and Amy Wynn shoot an air compressor hose into their mouths, blowing out their cheeks.

Faux Arrest: During the end credit shots, Paige is handcuffed by a local police officer.

Budget Boasting: Gen's total costs amount to $763 and some change—the lowest budget quoted on camera thus far in the series.

Gen's Room: ☺ ☺ ☹
Doug's Room: ☺ ☺ ☹

New York: Half Hollow Turn

Cast: Paige, Frank, Kia, Amy Wynn

The Rooms: Frank brings a living room up-to-date by painting the walls bamboo yellow, adding black accents on the walls and the furniture, using concrete stepping-stones to create side tables, converting a garden bench into a coffee table, and hanging a custom sculpture made from electrical and plumbing components. Kia gets funky in a basement rec room by painting the walls purple and light green, building a wall-length bench with purple velvet upholstery, hanging a swirly purple wallpaper border, installing halogen lights on a running cable, and creating green draperies.

Notable: This is theme queen Kia's first episode on the show.

Budget Crisis: Paige uses too much spray paint on Frank's concrete stepping-stone project, but Frank doesn't have the money to buy more paint.

Yum!: After the final Reveal, one of the homeowners presents a cake with the entire *Trading Spaces* cast airbrushed on the frosting.

Frank's Room: ☺ ☺ ☹
Kia's Room: ☺ ☺ ☹

Philadelphia: 22nd Street

Cast: Paige, Edward, Genevieve, Ty

The Rooms: Edward adds ethnic flair to a living room by painting the walls red, texturing the fireplace with black paint and tissue paper, hanging an existing rug on the wall, building a chaise lounge with finial feet, and installing an entertainment center made of shadow boxes. Gen heads to Cuba in a bedroom by covering the walls with textured white paint, adding a faux-plank finish to the doors, building a headboard enhanced with a blown-up image from a Cuban cigar box, designing lighted plastic bed tables, and creating picture frames out of cigar boxes.

Notable: Gen's inspiration for her room is the entire country of Cuba. She's never been.

Quotable Quote: Gen: "When you're working with a $1,000 budget, you've got to faux it up a bit."

Edward's Room: ☺ ☺ ☹
Gen's Room: ☺ ☺ ☹

Philadelphia: Gettysburg Lane
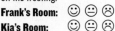

Cast: Paige, Frank, Vern, Ty

The Rooms: Frank updates a kitchen by painting the walls and cabinets several different colors, laying a stone-look vinyl tile, installing a new countertop, adding decorative elements to a half-wall to create a new serving bar, and mounting plates with wooden food cutouts across the soffit. Vern adds his version of cottage style to a living room by painting the walls yellow, installing white wainscoting,

building a 12-foot-wide shelving and storage unit, framing large copies of old family photos, making a "quilt" of images to hang above the storage unit, and adding touches of denim fabric throughout the room.

Fashion Report: Vern shows off his legs by wearing shorts.

Quotable Quote: Frank's male homeowner tries to get out of faux-finishing, suggesting that it's a job for a woman. Frank says, "All of a sudden I feel like I have to go out and buy a dress for the prom because I do this all the time."

Yawn: Vern gets virtually no sleep between Days 1 and 2 because he's trying to help finish the built-in storage unit.

Yucky Moments: Ty has a running gag of using wood glue as lotion, rubbing it into his hands, face, and neck.

Frank's Room: ☺ ☺ ☹
Vern's Room: ☺ ☺ ☹

Pennsylvania: Gorski Lane

Cast: Paige, Frank, Doug, Ty

The Rooms: Frank adds a celestial touch in a bedroom by painting the ceiling deep plum and painting silver stars across it. He paints the walls with several shades of cream and green, adds small blocks of color to the paneled doors, builds a writing desk, hangs a small cabinet upside down on the wall, and makes several pieces of custom artwork. Doug brings some "jungle boogie" to a bedroom by painting zebra stripes across all four walls, painting the ceiling dark brown, suspending a bamboo grid from the ceiling, and covering the existing headboard with sticks and bamboo.

Fashion Report: Doug shows off his legs by wearing shorts and flip-flops. There are also several buttons undone on his shirt.

Quotable Quote: When Frank unveils his purple paint, he says to his homeowners, "Prepare yourselves for the final squeal."

Oops!: While Ty is helping one of Frank's homeowners install a ceiling fan, Ty's drill falls from his ladder and lands on the fan, shattering the glass. (Ty eventually buys a new ceiling fan, paying for it himself so that it doesn't come out of Frank's budget.)

Conflict: One of Doug's homeowners is very concerned about covering the walls with zebra stripes. As she tries to talk him out of doing it, Doug says, "There's no way you're gonna stop me, so don't even try."

Resourceful: Doug wants to include a table but doesn't have extra money in his budget to pay for lumber. Ty ends up digging through the trash for scrap timber to make it.

Frank's Room: ☺ ☺ ☹
Doug's Room: ☺ ☺ ☹

Long Island: Dover Court ♥

Cast: Paige, Vern, Edward, Amy Wynn

The Rooms: Vern sets a boy's bedroom in motion by painting the walls various shades of blue, building a race car bed with working headlights, suspending a working train track and toy planes from the ceiling, and hanging a motorcycle swing made from recycled tires. Edward brings the outdoors into a bedroom by painting the walls moss green and antiquing a landscape print. He alters prefab side tables with filigreelike cuts, disguises ugly lamps with black spray paint and fabric slipcovers, hangs antique glass shutters over the windows, and builds a large entertainment center, using the existing side tables and glass shutters.

Notable: Vern's homeowner keeps saying "sweet," and Vern tries to claim the word is his.

Resourceful: Having heard that Vern is doing a "planes, trains, and automobiles" room, neighborhood kids want to give him pictures of all three to hang in the room. Vern likes the idea but points out that he doesn't have the money to pay them. The kids donate the pictures, which Vern then incorporates into the room.

Confession Time: While sewing, Edward's male homeowner admits that his wife is better than he is with power tools.

Vern's Room: ☺ ☺ ☹
Edward's Room: ☺ ☺ ☹

Pennsylvania: Victoria Drive

Cast: Paige, Doug, Kia, Amy Wynn

The Rooms: Doug creates a cabin feel in a living room by covering the walls in brown Venetian plaster, hanging red Roman shades, covering a prefab coffee table with leather, staining the existing sofa and coffee tables, sewing cowprint pillows, building a large armoire covered with rough-cut poplar, and hanging leftover lumber on the walls in decorative stripes. Kia creates her version of an indoor garden in a guest bedroom by painting the walls yellow, hanging a flowery wallpaper border on the ceiling, creating a duvet out of synthetic turf and silk flowers, building a headboard from a tree limb, hanging a chair swing from a cedar arbor, placing gravel under the swing, and building a picket fence room divider.

Fashion Report: In keeping with the theme of her room, Kia wears overalls and a straw hat.

Yucky Moment: When Doug's homeowners enter the room to meet him at the start of the show, Doug is barefoot and enjoying a plate of brownies. Doug offers to share, but his team turns down the offer because Doug's feet are close to the plate. Doug then taps his foot across the top of the brownies and offers them again.

Quotable Quote: Doug defends his dark stain choice by saying, "I would not damage anything of quality. I only damage things that are crappy."

Impressive Impersonation: Kia does her best Gary Coleman by saying, "Wha'choo talkin' 'bout, Amy Wynn?"

Doug's Room: ☺ ☺ ☹
Kia's Room: ☺ ☺ ☹

New Jersey: Manitoba Trail

Cast: Paige, Frank, Doug, Amy Wynn

The Rooms: Frank goes all out in a country living/dining room by painting the walls light green, distressing the floors, painting a faux rug under the coffee table, applying several decorative paint colors and finishes to an antique cabinet, building custom lamps with large antique yarn spools, and creating three homemade country-girl dolls out of pillow forms. Doug brightens a living room by painting everything—the walls, ceiling, ceiling beams, fireplace, and ceiling fans—bright white ("White Whoa"). He buys two new white sofas, hangs bright blue draperies, installs a new doorbell that blends into the white wall, sews many brightly colored throw pillows, makes a large framed mirror, and creates custom art pieces.

Foot Fetish: Doug goes barefoot while painting a white border on a natural rug and puts his bare feet near his female homeowner's head while she sews pillows.

Reveal-ing Moment: The male living/dining room homeowner is so happy about his room that he kisses Paige.

Frank's Room: ☺ ☺ ☹
Doug's Room: ☺ ☺ ☹

Nazareth: First Street

Cast: Paige, Vern, Doug, Amy Wynn

The Rooms: Vern adds a touch of serenity to a living room by painting three walls taupe and one wall deep blue, adding a new mantel, sewing throw pillows with a wave motif, suspending mini symbiotic environments from the ceiling, building a coffee table with a center inset of sand and candles, and placing six fountains around the fireplace. Doug gives a kitchen an earthy feel by laying brown peel-and-stick vinyl flooring, painting the walls beige, making new orange laminate countertops, painting the cabinets yellow with an orange glaze, adding crown molding to the cabinet tops, building a pie safe, and upholstering the dining chairs with red-orange fabric.

Fashion Report: Vern's pants fall down as he's running during the opening segment.

Notable: Amy Wynn and Doug have a food fight during the end credits.

Vern's Room: ☺ ☹ ☹

Doug's Room: ☺ ☹ ☹

New Jersey: Catania Court ⑤

Cast: Paige, Hildi, Genevieve, Amy Wynn

The Rooms: Hildi has the golden touch in a bedroom: She paints the walls yellow-green, sews bedding with fabrics she purchased in India, uses batik-inspired stamps to create gold accents on the ceiling and around the room, replaces the existing baseboards with taller ones, adds a gold wash to the existing furniture, builds a low-slung "opium couch," and hangs a vintage glass light fixture. Gen finds the silver lining in a dining room: She paints the walls carnelian red, hangs silver crown molding, paints the trim and chair rail ivory, hangs ivory and silver draperies, paints a canvas floorcloth to lay under the table, and hangs a new light fixture that has small tree limbs attached to it.

Fashion Report: Hildi's male homeowner starts the show wearing heels, noting that he's chosen "Hildi-approved footwear." Hildi paints his toenails with the room paint. When the homeowner starts to take off the shoes in order to paint, Hildi tells him to put them back on, pointing out that she never goes barefoot on the job.

Ringing Inspiration: Gen gets her design idea from a piece of her own jewelry, a ring that came from Afghanistan.

Hildi's Room: ☺ ☹ ☹

Gen's Room: ☺ ☹ ☹

Philadelphia: East Avenue ⑦

Cast: Paige, Hildi, Frank, Amy Wynn

The Rooms: Hildi gets graphic in a living room by painting three walls yellow, covering one wall with a large Lichtenstein-inspired portrait of herself, adding a glass-shelf bar area, building all new tables and chairs, sewing cushions with mod pink and orange fabric, and re-covering a thrift store couch with red fabric. Frank brightens a living room by painting the walls deep purple, painting the ceiling bright red, designing a coffee table unit with four bases that move apart and become extra seating, and creating wall art with rain gutter materials and round wooden cutouts.

Notable: All four homeowners are members of the Philadelphia Charge, a professional women's soccer team.

Resourceful: After applying one coat of purple paint on the wall, Frank realizes that the original burgundy paint is showing through in patches, creating an unexpected faux finish. He decides to keep it that way.

Quotable Quote: While hanging draperies, Frank dispenses his wisdom, saying, "A little fluffing is good."

Reveal-ing Moments: The homeowners are "weirded out" by the Hildi portrait in their living room.

Hildi's Room: ☺ ☹ ☹

Frank's Room: ☺ ☹ ☹

Virginia: Gentle Heights Court ⑤ ♥

Cast: Paige, Hildi, Kia, Ty

The Rooms: Hildi roughs it in a boy's bedroom by painting the walls and ceiling midnight blue, hanging a moon-shape light fixture, placing glow-in-the-dark stars on the ceiling, hanging a solar system mobile, building a 13-foot rock climbing wall, adding fold-up camping furniture, placing the mattress in a room-size tent, using a blue sleeping bag as a duvet, and placing camping lanterns around the room. Kia adds sensuous details to a bedroom by painting the walls orange, painting the trim Grecian blue, hanging a red and gold wallpaper border, creating a Taj Mahal cutout to place around the existing entertainment center, installing two

---

wooden columns from India, adding bedding made from sari fabrics, and suspending the bed from the ceiling with chains.

Guy Stuff: Ty (wearing a bike helmet for safety, of course) tries out the completed rock wall, falling to the floor.

Quotable Quote: When Kia asks Ty when he's going to hang the chains for her bed, he says, "Just as soon as you're through yanking mine."

Notable: A shirtless Ty suns himself during the end credits.

Reveal-ing Moments: Upon seeing the suspended bed in her newly decorated room, the female homeowner exclaims, "I wanna jump in there and get naked!"

Hildi's Room: ☺ ☹ ☹

Kia's Room: ☺ ☹ ☹

Arlington: First Road 💣   ⑦

Cast: Paige, Hildi, Doug, Ty

The Rooms: Hildi gift-wraps a bedroom by painting the walls "Tiffany box" aqua blue, adding a duvet and Roman shades in the same aqua blue, airbrushing white "ribbons" on the walls and fabrics, hanging white lamps with square shades above the headboard, building acrylic side tables that light up from inside, and adding bright silver accents. Doug warms up a bedroom by painting the walls and ceiling a deep gray-blue, hanging white Roman shades with brown silk curtains and cornice boards, constructing a headboard from a large existing window frame, balancing the headboard with a new armoire that features white silk door insets, and creating custom artwork in brown and navy.

Homework Blunder: For homework, Hildi has her team airbrush the "ribbons" on the walls. When she returns on Day 2, the project is complete but not quite the way she would have done it. (The "ribbons" are very large and look more like Keith Haring-inspired graffiti.)

Notable: One of Hildi's homeowners leaves an apology note on the wall in black marker. It says, "Hildi made me do it."

Conflict: Doug's homeowners fight him on every decision, including removing the ceiling fan, selecting paint colors, painting the ceiling, staining the floor, and accessorizing the room. Near the end of Day 1, Doug washes his hands of the room and uses the PaigeCam to record instructions for making draperies. Paige then takes the camera to the homeowners and helps them make the curtains.

Quotable Quote: At a heated point in the conflict with his homeowners, Doug exclaims, "I can't continue to educate people on what's good taste!"

Reconciliation?: While Doug is reclining in a lawn chair reading a newspaper, his homeowners come to say that they need him after all. By the end of Day 2, Doug's female homeowner admits that the design is growing on her. Doug says, "It's growing on her like a fungus, but it's growing."

Hildi's Room: ☺ ☹ ☹

Doug's Room: ☺ ☹ ☹

Washington, D.C.: Quebec Place

Cast: Paige, Genevieve, Vern, Ty

The Rooms: Gen dishes up a serene living room inspired by her favorite Thai soup. She paints the walls a light bone color and gives the room lemongrass green accents, a newly constructed sofa, a wall-length valance with lemongrass curtains, and lotus flower light fixtures. Vern turns up the heat in a newlywed couple's bedroom by painting the fireplace and dressing room red, installing a floor-to-ceiling mirrored wall in the dressing area, hanging rows of crystals above the fireplace, sewing red silk Roman blinds, and installing a large headboard with red silk insets.

Fashion Report: High heels abound in this episode: Both female homeowners wear them during the Key Swap and the Reveal; Gen wears them when first meeting the homeowners. Comfort and practicality win out, and everyone

---

quickly removes the shoes.

Notable: This episode is the first time Kia's and Edward's faces appear among the quick shots of the designers during the opening credits.

Oops!: When Ty attempts to install a wall-length valance he built for Gen's room, he discovers that he built it 1 foot too long. Much discussion ensues, and Ty eventually cuts 6 inches from each end.

Well, Thanks: Gen liberally hands out kudos, telling Ty that the couch he built is her favorite piece of furniture he's created during the series. She also tells her homeowners that their stain job on the sofa frame is the best anyone has done on the show.

Head Games: Vern's headboard is so large and unwieldy that he has to have a police car stop traffic so that he and his homeowner can carry it across the street. After they get it inside, they find it's too large to go up a flight of stairs, and Ty has to cut length off the bottom to fix the situation.

Resourceful: Vern initially planned to restore the hardwood floor in his room, but by the end of Day 2, he shows Paige the large red rug he has purchased to hide the floor, which is not shaping up as he had hoped.

Reveal-ing Moments: The male homeowner on one of the teams is so happy, he kisses Paige on both cheeks. His wife likes the makeover so much, she says she doesn't even care that he's kissing another woman.

Gen's Room: ☺ ☹ ☹

Vern's Room: ☺ ☹ ☹

Indiana: River Valley Drive

Cast: Paige, Doug, Genevieve, Amy Wynn

The Rooms: Gen tones down an overly bright living room by painting the walls a sleek silver-gray, painting existing furniture white, designing a new entertainment center made out of stacked white boxes with punched-aluminum door insets, and adding a few bold touches of color with green curtains, a new green room screen, and a fuchsia ottoman. Doug puts his foot down in his "Back from Brazil" living room, hanging a three-section painting of his own foot. He also stencils white flowers—inspired by sarongs—on the walls, slipcovers the existing furniture in white, extends the fireplace mantel, designs an acrylic plastic light fixture, and sews throw pillows out of tie-dyed sarongs.

Ouch!: During B-roll footage, Gen bounces a basketball off her head as if it were a soccer ball. Doug looks concerned and kisses her forehead.

Musical Moment: Gen plays guitar for Amy Wynn during the end credits, making up a song about kicking Amy Wynn's butt if she doesn't finish her carpentry projects. She's a little off-key.

Huh?: Doug's original stencil idea takes too long, and he has to design another one that he thinks will be easier. It isn't. During the Reveal, the homeowners seem confused by the stenciling and ask, "What is that? An olive?"

Gen's Room: ☺ ☹ ☹

Doug's Room: ☺ ☹ ☹

Indiana: Fieldhurst Lane

Cast: Paige, Doug, Vern, Amy Wynn

The Rooms: Doug gets back to his Midwestern roots in a bedroom by painting the walls orange, installing padded tan wainscoting, creating custom paintings of wheat and corn, embellishing simple white bedding with orange ribbon and yarn, and designing a large armoire. Vern sets a restful scene in a bedroom by painting the walls a light blue, attaching oak plywood squares to a wall, painting

169

the existing furniture black, reupholstering a chaise longue with dark blue velvet, hanging blue velvet draperies, wrapping the bed frame with white beaded garland, and installing new sconces and a ceiling fixture with white beaded shades.

Farm Fun: During the opening, Doug drives a tractor, Paige milks a cow, and Vern and Amy Wynn put up hay bales.

Name Game: Doug gets a little confused about the name of his room, calling it at various times "Sunset Harvest," "Harvest Sunset," "Indian Sunset," and "Golden Harvest"—all of which are Doug-speak for orange.

Joke Time: At the start of Day 2, Doug tells his homeowners that he doesn't like the bright orange walls and that they're going to have to repaint them light green. Paige tells Doug no, Doug insists, and they storm off arguing. Doug reenters with brushes and starts painting a wall himself. When the homeowners finally relent and pick up brushes, Doug laughs and says, "Gotcha!" His female homeowner gets the last laugh though, slapping Doug's face with her green paint-covered brush.

Hair Care: During the end credits, Paige points out Vern's emerging bald spot.

Kiss-Off: When Paige says goodbye at the end of the show, all four homeowners blow a kiss toward the camera à la *The Dating Game.*

Doug's Room: ☺ 😐 ☹
Vern's Room: ☺ 😐 ☹

Indiana: Halleck Way

Cast: Paige, Edward, Kia, Amy Wynn

The Rooms: Edward designs a soft yet masculine bedroom by painting the tray ceiling slate blue and white, painting the walls and existing furniture tan, hanging a customized light fixture with a hand-painted glass frame, draping white fabric across the length of one wall, hanging lush brown draperies, and slipcovering the head- and footboards. He also rearranges the furniture and creates neoclassic wall shelves. Kia walks like an Egyptian in a bedroom by painting the walls "Tut Wine" and "Pharaoh Gold," building pyramid-shape cornice boards, and hanging framed Egyptian prints and a handmade Eye of Horace. She also paints a personalized hieroglyphic message for the homeowners ("David loves Noel") on an existing room screen and installs a ceiling fan with palm leaves attached to the blades.

Vroom: Edward and Kia drive a race car at the Indianapolis Motor Speedway.

Quotable Quote: Toward the end of Day 2, Edward tells Paige that the room is "kind of coming together." Paige responds by saying, "Yeah, if you stress the words 'kind of.'"

Diva Fit!: Early in Day 1, Kia's homeowners run out of paint during the first coat. Kia blames the homeowners' painting ability; Paige blames Kia's paint calculations. Kia eventually gives the homeowners a painting lesson in an attempt to salvage what paint she has left. They wind up having to buy another gallon.

Scare Flair: During a bumper shot, Paige enters wrapped up in toilet paper like a mummy.

Ouch!: When Kia discovers her male homeowner and Amy Wynn installing cornice boards without installing the curtain rods first, she takes a piece of fabric, wraps it around the homeowner's neck, and pretends to strangle him.

Fountain Follies: Kia spends much of her budget on a pyramid-shape fountain that she designed herself. The fountain is the subject of many discussions, including questions about its construction, sealant, and pump mechanism (Amy Wynn works on this while squatting in the homeowners' water-filled bathtub). Late on Day 2, Kia and her team meet up with Amy Wynn and an obviously leaky

fountain; they decide to chuck the whole thing at the last minute.

Edward's Room: ☺ 😐 ☹
Kia's Room: ☺ 😐 ☹

Missouri: Sunburst Drive

Cast: Paige, Genevieve, Vern, Ty

The Rooms: Gen draws inspiration for a bedroom from gauchos, Argentine cowboys: She paints the walls deep brown, creates faux crown molding, installs a woven leather-and-red-velvet headboard, and glues pictures of gauchos to the closet doors. She also builds an upholstered bench and pulls in furniture from other rooms. Vern adds a masculine edge to a girlie bedroom by painting the walls soft blue, painting the existing furniture and doors red, designing a wall-length desk and computer hutch, installing a headboard made of upholstered leather squares, and adding several Moroccan wrought-iron light fixtures and accents.

Fashion Report: The cast members wear monogrammed bowling shirts and bowl during the B-roll footage. Gen bowls barefoot.

Quotable Quote: When Gen's female homeowner mentions that she's nervous about her own room, Gen reassures her by saying, "Do you like clean lines and straight things? Vern does."

Silly Gen!: Paige chastises Gen and her team for falling behind on Day 1, asking them what they've gotten done. Gen sheepishly replies, "We've laughed a lot."

More Gen: While working with her female homeowner to upholster a bench, Gen shows her how to use cardboard to keep a straight, professional-looking line when finishing off the edges. She then says jokingly under her breath, "Because that's all we are on this show—a bunch of professionals."

Gen's Room: ☺ 😐 ☹
Vern's Room: ☺ 😐 ☹

Scott Air Force Base: Ash Creek

Cast: Paige, Doug, Kia, Ty

The Rooms: Doug travels down Route 66 in a child's bedroom by laying gray carpet, painting highway stripes and road signs on the walls, and installing a front and back end from two actual cars. (He adds a mattress in the back end of one car, and the front end of the other car serves as a toy chest.) Kia creates "Military Chic" in a living/dining room, using various shades of gray paint, new chair rails, a gray and white camouflage wallpaper border, pillows and cushions in the same camouflage, a new storage bench, a faux fireplace, a red slipcover, red accents, and draperies made from a gray parachute.

Take It Easy: During Load Out, Doug sits in a child's chair as his homeowners do all the work. They eventually carry the chair out of the room—with Doug in it.

Family Ties: As Doug reveals his design idea to Ty, a Wilson Trucking semi drives up loaded with the two car halves. It then becomes an act from a circus, as seven people start filing out of the cab. Doug introduces them as his brothers, nephews, and friends—all of whom are there to help carry the car halves around.

Car-nival: Getting the cars into the room is insanely difficult and time-consuming. The front end doesn't fit down the hallway and has to be sawed in half and reassembled inside the room. Ty spends so much time on Doug's cars that he has to cut one of Kia's projects.

Drop In: Kia meets her homeowners after having supposedly parachuted onto the roof.

Shocking Confession: Kia admits to her female homeowner that she's "never used a slipcover before."

Fashion Report: During Designer Chat, Kia wears an outfit that seems to consist of several layers of multicolor printed fabrics. It boggles the mind.

Doug's Room: ☺ 😐 ☹
Kia's Room: ☺ 😐 ☹

Missouri: Sweetbriar Lane

Cast: Paige, Edward, Frank, Ty

The Rooms: Edward designs a sleek bedroom by painting the walls shades of gray, white, and China blue, adding extra closet and storage space, and designing a mirrored entertainment armoire to hide the TV. He also hangs a light fixture wrapped in pearls, adds gray, purple, blue, and green fabrics, and creates a sculpture out of curled metal. Frank creates an unusual bedroom, painting the walls orange and installing large eyes made of copper tubing above the bed. An upholstered lip headboard completes the face, and a new platform bed stands beneath it. Frank paints the fireplace purple and creates an artistic theme by installing a giant pencil on one wall and painting sketches of women around it.

Edward's Design Theory: "I always think you need a touch of black in a room."

Heavy Metal: Gushing about his metal sculpture during Designer Chat, Edward tells Paige that he wants to make more pieces like it because he enjoyed the sparks flying when he sawed into the metal.

Ouch?: During the Carpenter Consult, Frank jokingly knocks Ty to the ground. Ty milks the experience by wearing a neck brace for the rest of the show and acting as though he's in constant pain anytime he's near Frank.

Southern Belle: When Paige jokes about the layered tulle "petticoat" lampshades that Frank has designed, Frank smugly admits, "During the Civil War, I used to make 'em for the troops."

Quotable Quote: Frank tells Paige that he used her lips as inspiration for his headboard. She's impressed that he noticed her lips, and he replies, "I may be old, but I'm not dead."

Frank the Vampire Slayer? During the end credits, an extended shot of Frank shows him carving the giant pencil out of a piece of unpainted wood. Frank tells the camera that he's making a vampire stake and cautions viewers to be careful who they stake, because "anyone walking around after dawn is not a vampire."

Edward's Room: ☺ 😐 ☹
Frank's Room: ☺ 😐 ☹

London: Garden Flat

Cast: Paige, Genevieve, Hildi, Handy Andy of *Changing Rooms*

The Rooms: Gen enlivens a bedroom by painting the walls a rich, spicy orange, painting a small alcove red, and hanging many yellow-green draperies. She builds a new platform bed with drawers underneath, adds a prefab dresser, and creates an unusual closet space along one wall. She also installs crown molding and hangs rows of framed Chinese newsprint. Hildi brightens a girls' bedroom by splattering bright paint on white walls, laying fluffy white carpet, framing the girls' artwork, and sewing rainbow-color draperies. She also installs doors on an existing wall-size shelving unit, builds beds and nightstands on casters, and creates a "secret garden" area with wheat grass plants.

Notable: This is the first "International Challenge" between *Trading Spaces* and its sister show, *Changing Rooms.*

Dialect Differences: Paige mangles a British accent repeatedly and, not surprisingly, has major trouble understanding Handy Andy. Later, Gen tries to explain the concept of crown molding to Handy Andy, who eventually explains that the British call the same thing "coving."

Weather Woes: Gale-force winds upset the show on Day 2, blowing the Carpentry World tent into a neighboring yard. Gen, Paige, and Handy Andy jump over the neighbor's fence and try to put the tent back into place. After getting it back in the right spot, but not getting it to stand up completely, Handy Andy turns to the two giggling women and dismisses them, saying, "You've annoyed me enough now."

More Weather Woes: While struggling with the tent, Handy Andy points out that the old slate tiles on nearby roofs may blow off and hit people below. This seriously upsets Paige, who decides to move the prefab dresser assembly project inside.

Messy Madam: After throwing paint on the walls, Hildi is completely covered in paint (a *Trading Spaces* first?). She apparently didn't remember her own advice to a paint-covered Dez in Lawrenceville: Pine Lane (Season I): "Delegate, delegate, delegate!"

Yucky Moment: When Hildi asks whether she's gotten all the paint off her face, Paige gleefully informs her that a spot of yellow paint in the middle of Hildi's nose resembles a "whitehead zit." Hildi is grossed out.

Hildi's Room: ☺ ☺ ☹
Gen's Room: ☺ ☺ ☹

Mississippi: Golden Pond

Cast: Paige, Laurie, Hildi, Amy Wynn

The Rooms: Laurie updates a bedroom by painting the walls camel-yellow, building a large headboard of upholstered aqua fabric with a chocolate brown grid overlay, creating a large mirror from smaller mirrored squares, hanging a thrift store chandelier, adding newly upholstered thrift store chairs, using aqua and camel-yellow bedding, and building new chocolate brown bookcases. Hildi adds color to a bathroom (a *Trading Spaces* first!) by stapling more than 6,000 silk flowers to the walls, painting the trim and cabinets gold, creating red acrylic cabinet door insets, building a bench upholstered in terry cloth, and sewing draperies and a shower curtain out of floral fabrics from France.

Notable: This is Laurie's first episode back after maternity leave. Baby Gibson makes a quick appearance on the morning of Day 2.

Tub Time: While sitting (apparently naked) in a tub full of bubbles, the bathroom homeowners describe what they'd like to see done to their room.

Ouch!: Laurie's male homeowner injured his foot by driving his motorcycle into a building. He tells Paige that it was a learning experience, much like *Trading Spaces*, adding that *Trading Spaces* is "slightly more interesting and almost as painful" as hitting that wall.

For Laughs: Laurie is in high spirits this episode, hula-hooping during a bumper shot, doing a bad approximation of a New Jersey accent during the end credits, and doing her best impression of an upholstered headboard for her homeowners.

Hildi's Room: ☺ ☺ ☹
Laurie's Room: ☺ ☺ ☹

Mississippi: Winsmere Way

Cast: Paige, Laurie, Hildi, Amy Wynn

The Rooms: Laurie spices up the bedroom of a newly divorced homeowner with cumin yellow walls, an eggplant

---

ceiling, a large upholstered headboard with nailhead trim, a new chaise lounge, a blown-glass light fixture, and two upholstered message boards. Hildi adds drama to a bedroom by covering the walls in red toile fabric, painting the ceiling smoky plum, slipcovering a thrift store sofa with cream fabric, building a new armoire with curved doors, repainting two thrift store lamps, and creating shadow boxes.

Deco-Dramas: Laurie has some traumatic moments during the episode. Her purple ceiling isn't quite the eggplant shade she had hoped for (she calls it "Disco '70s Nightmare" and goes out to find new paint). Later, Laurie doesn't have enough ribbon to create her message boards. Her homeowners save the day by designing a new pattern for the ribbon. Laurie gushes that she's so glad when she has smart homeowners.

More Deco-Dramas: Laurie's "smart homeowners" have moments of their own though: While hanging two towel bars that act as magazine racks, they nearly destroy the wall trying to put in wall anchors and can't seem to get the racks level. During the end credits there is a shot of them working on this project, and the male homeowner says, "They don't show the real-life crap."

Lounge Act: Laurie states that the chaise is the best piece Amy Wynn has ever built for her and points out that "every Southern woman needs a chaise longue."

Oops!: While attaching the toile fabric to the walls, Hildi accidentally shoots a staple at Paige's rear end. It doesn't go in, but Paige notices it.

Hildi's Design Theory: "I can see the beauty in many things."

Under Where? When she begins to glaze a dresser, Hildi opens the drawers to find that they hadn't been emptied. The top drawer is full of underwear, which Hildi grabs by the handful and throws at her homeowners. One homeowner exclaims, "It's raining panties!"

Hildi's Room: ☺ ☺ ☹
Laurie's Room: ☺ ☺ ☹

San Antonio: Ghostbridge

Cast: Paige, Hildi, Vern, Ty

The Rooms: Hildi gets groovy in a living room by lining one wall with record albums and painting the remaining walls purple, yellow, teal, and orange. She creates slipcovers in the same colors, makes a coffee table top by covering a colorful scarf with a large piece of glass, paints the homeowners' favorite chair black with brightly colored flowers, installs lamps made from French drainpipes, and designs a large entertainment center. Vern leaves his mark in a living room by covering one wall with wood veneer wallpaper, bringing in new pieces of brown furniture, hanging red draperies, creating a red and gold leaf coffee table and room screen, and laying a red rug.

Notable: Hildi refers to herself as "the Slipcover Queen."

Happy Feet: When Ty and Hildi's male homeowner bring in the base for the entertainment center, Hildi jumps on it and starts dancing before they've had a chance to put it down.

Dream Team?: Vern refers to his homeowners and himself as the "Obsessive-Compulsive Disorder Triplets." His homeowners agree.

Attraction Action: One of Vern's homeowners has a serious crush on Vern and Ty. During the episode, she hits on both Ty and Vern, protects Vern from criticism, and refers to Vern as "my Vern."

Reveal-ing Moment: The album room homeowner isn't sure about her room and keeps repeating, "This is...unique."

Hildi's Room: ☺ ☺ ☹
Vern's Room: ☺ ☺ ☹

Austin: Wyoming Valley Drive

Cast: Paige, Laurie, Hildi, Ty

The Rooms: Laurie adds warmth to a dining room by weaving one wall with brown sueded cotton and painting the other walls pink-orange. She builds a round dining table with a stenciled top and a fabric skirt, designs a buffet table with legs made from plumbing conduit, and makes draperies and seat cushions out of green fabric. Hildi creates a sleek kitchen by covering the walls with peel-and-stick wine labels, painting the cabinets black, deepening an existing bench, designing a large pot rack out of lumber and copper plumbing conduit, painting the existing wooden blinds black and orange, slipcovering the dining chairs with orange fabric, and embellishing the dining table with gold accents.

Quotable Quote: Paige asks the dining room homeowners what they're afraid of finding when they return home. The female homeowner says that she doesn't want any type of neon color, and Paige replies sarcastically, "Yeah, because Laurie is known for neon."

Design Differences: An ongoing debate about whether the kitchen homeowners will like having more than 4,000 wine labels stuck to their walls consumes much of the episode. Their neighbors continually point out that the homeowners don't drink or keep any type of alcohol in their home. Hildi adjusts her vision a bit, converting her design for a wine rack into a pot rack, but the wine labels stay.

Hildi's Design Theory: "I try to show people different things to do with the obvious."

Reveal-ing Moment: The kitchen homeowners aren't thrilled with the labels. Their neighbors enter the room at the end of the show with a steamer, tied with a ribbon, that can be used to remove the labels.

Hildi's Room: ☺ ☺ ☹
Laurie's Room: ☺ ☺ ☹

Austin: Aire Libre Drive

Cast: Paige, Frank, Kia, Ty

The Rooms: Frank adds drama to a living room by painting one wall orange and the other walls yellow, building two new end tables, designing a massive coffee table out of a black granite slab and four decorative columns, adding a toy chest to hold the homeowners' dog toys, covering the existing furniture with multicolor fabric, and laying a new rug. Kia updates a living room by painting the walls moss and brown, painting a golden glaze on the brown wall, designing new draperies out of various types of printed fabric, building a large frame above the fireplace, adding a new love seat, and scavenging accessories from other rooms in the house.

Fashion Report: The cowboy hat officially becomes the most common *Trading Spaces* fashion accessory, with Paige donning one in the Opener.

Budget Crisis: Frank is already $123 over budget when his homeowners meet him on Day I. He manages to return enough things over the course of the show that he's under budget by Designer Chat.

Yucky Moment: While trying to hang Kia's mirror, Ty accidentally breaks the wire on the back of the frame. As Paige is trying to decide what to do, Ty pretends to floss Paige's teeth with the broken wire. (He evidently didn't hear Doug's warning about this practice in Philadelphia: Valley Road.)

Lazy Days: Because Kia and Frank's combined carpentry load takes only a few minutes to complete, Ty decides to organize and clean the *Trading Spaces* trailer and enlists the help of neighborhood kids. One of Kia's homeowners wants to work with Ty even though Ty

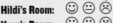

171

doesn't have anything to do, so Ty pretends to teach him to use a broom. During Day 2, Frank finds Ty relaxing in a hot tub. Paige feels so sorry for Ty, she lets him call Time's Up.

Mad Dash: Kia summarizes her design philosophy for the room as "redecorating by relocating." During the Hurry-Up sequence, Kia and her homeowners run around the house finding items to accessorize the room. Kia and her female homeowner find several items, but the male homeowner returns with only an unattractive Mardi Gras-theme egg.

Last Laughs: During the end credits, Paige rides Ty like a horse; Ty demonstrates his pole-vaulting ability with a piece of Kia's lumber, breaking the board in midair.

Frank's Room: ☺ 😐 ☹
Kia's Room: ☺ 😐 ☹

Austin: Wampton Way

Cast: Paige, Genevieve, Doug, Ty

The Rooms: Gen adds an Art Deco touch to a living room by color-washing the walls in various shades of yellow and orange, slipcovering the existing furniture with graphic black and white fabric, building up the existing fireplace with black and mahogany accents, suspending the television with cables and a wooden shelf, adding two large topiaries, and framing various champagne and liqueur posters. Doug gives a living room an antique Spanish flair by building a large dark brown fireplace facade, painting the walls smoky green, and staining existing barstools darker brown. He adds a chair upholstered in newspaper-print fabric and creates wall art with canvas and newspapers.

Sideshow: Theatrical weirdness abounds during the Opener: Gen, Doug, and Ty wear costumes and bad wigs while performing a magic trick (Doug cuts Ty in half with a chain saw while Gen strikes poses). Paige makes herself disappear.

Attraction Action?: When entering the room for the first time, Gen's male homeowner (who works as a stand-up comedian) says to Ty, "Man, Ty, you *are* hot!"

Name Game: For no apparent reason, Doug's male homeowner calls him "Sparky."

Quotable Quote: Gen's female homeowner has never made a slipcover but admits that she made three Jedi Halloween costumes for her kids. Gen's reply: "Jedi costumes equal slipcovers to me."

Musical Moment: Doug plays trombone in a bumper shot.

Surprise!: During Load Out, Gen's team removes the existing sectional couch and finds a body outline underneath, planted as a joke by the homeowners.

Yucky Moment #1: Gen's male homeowner, who's been known to streak, goes outside to work with Ty wearing nothing but a tool belt and strategically placed paint chips. Noting that Ty is flustered, the homeowner suggests coming back later, turns to walk away, and exposes his rear to the camera.

More Yucky Moments: Gen's homeowners suggest that instead of buying rags, they could use their neighbors' underwear to apply the color wash to the walls. Later, PaigeCam footage shows Gen digging through the male homeowner's underwear drawer. Gen presents the selected boxers to her team and proceeds to wear a pair on her head. Her team follows suit.

Show Time: Gen tests the strength of the suspended entertainment shelf by dancing on it. Ty and Gen's male homeowner give her dollar bills.

Waterworks?: Paige asks Doug whether redoing the fireplace will upset the homeowners (referring to Seattle: 137th Street in Season 2). Doug assures Paige that these homeowners will "only cry tears of joy."

Fashion Report: During Designer Chat Gen wears the same dress as the woman in one of the champagne posters used for design inspiration.

Doug's Design Theory: "Every room has to have a little quirk in it."

Gen's Room: ☺ 😐 ☹
Doug's Room: ☺ 😐 ☹

San Diego: Camino Mojado ☹

Cast: Paige, Vern, Genevieve, Ty

The Rooms: Gen adds Polynesian flair to a bedroom by building a grass-cloth headboard, hanging mosquito netting, painting the walls smoky taupe, painting the existing furniture orange, sewing two new dog beds out of the same material as the new bedspread, planting several large palm plants, and building a large square shelving unit to hold accessories and a TV. Vern cozies up a loft TV room by attaching several upholstered diamond shapes on two walls, building new black velvet sofas, designing a large black coffee table with upholstered panels, framing photocopies of Hollywood movie legends on vellum, installing new shelving to hold entertainment equipment, and hanging several black and taupe drapery panels to close off the room.

Notable: Gen admits that she's allergic to dogs.

Oops!: Gen's grass-cloth headboard completely falls apart when Ty and Gen's female homeowner try to move it off a construction table.

Farm Fetish?: When Gen's homeowners tell her that they're not really worried about what Vern may be doing to their home, Gen jokes that Vern has been wanting to explore new design avenues, including "the barnyard look." Oddly enough, the next scene shows Vern telling his female homeowner to stuff a pillow as she would stuff a turkey.

Cabinet Chaos: Ty changes Gen's cabinet design, adding several time-consuming decorative elements. The piece isn't finished by the morning of Day 2, and Gen asks Ty to finish building the piece and add the decorative elements later if he has time. Later, Paige finds Ty doing decorative work on the uncompleted piece; she reads him the riot act. Ty eventually finishes the piece at the last minute, only to find that it's too big to be easily carried up the stairs.

Vern's Room: ☺ 😐 ☹
Gen's Room: ☺ 😐 ☹

San Diego: Dusty Trail

Cast: Paige, Doug, Genevieve, Ty

The Rooms: Doug designs a bedroom he calls "Cosmo Shab" by color-washing the walls with three shades of blue paint, painting the cathedral ceiling gray, installing crown molding, hanging a chandelier from the dining room, sewing gray and white toile draperies, painting the existing furniture white, and distressing the newly painted pieces to create an antique look. Gen transforms a kitchen into a French *boucherie* (butcher shop) by covering the walls with green chalkboard paint, painting the cabinets vanilla with gray insets, installing a tin ceiling, building a larger tabletop, and hanging pictures of "meat puppets" around the room.

Fashion Report: The cast members wear wet suits, and Ty successfully surfs during B-roll footage.

Mini Diva Fit: Paige tells Doug's female homeowner, "You have perfect teeth." Doug is put out that Paige doesn't say the same about him.

New Toy: Doug and Ty have fun with a new piece of equipment—a laser-pointer level that is the size of a large tape measure.

Baby Boom: As she hands a respirator mask to her pregnant female homeowner, Gen says, "This paint is a little bit toxic, and I want your baby to be born with all its fingers and toes." She then cites Ty as an example of what could happen to the woman's child if she doesn't wear a mask.

Kudos: Gen says of Doug, "He might have a lot of attitude, but he's a damn fine designer."

Tardy Tin: The tin for Gen's ceiling doesn't arrive until the morning of Day 2, after getting stuck somewhere in Nebraska. Because Ty has to work on Doug's house, Gen's male homeowner installs the tin himself. For the Reveal, most of the tin is installed, with the exception of a small strip at the edge of the room. Gen informs viewers, "Tin is not a two-day project, just so you know."

French Flair: Gen wears a beret during Designer Chat and says, "Ooh la la, my room rocks!"

Quotable Quote: When the female bedroom homeowner sees her room, she says, "I feel so bad for saying all that bad stuff about Doug!"

Gen's Room: ☺ 😐 ☹
Doug's Room: ☺ 😐 ☹

San Diego: Fairfield ❓ 👶 🔧 ☹

Cast: Paige, Kia, Frank, Ty

The Rooms: Kia updates an office/game room by painting the walls apricot and the trim orange. She builds a strange love seat that sits 8 inches off the ground, designs a removable tabletop for an existing game table, builds storage cubes that double as seats, hangs a "mirror" made of CDs, makes chess pieces out of copper pipe, and rearranges the existing desk to create a more effective office area. Frank fluffs a "tranquil love nest" in a bedroom, adding coffee-color paint, a new coffee bar (complete with a small refrigerator), wooden chevrons on the existing furniture, gauzy fabric draped around the four-poster bed, and a large piece of bamboo for a drapery rod.

Oops!: Frank's male homeowner bought new shoes for the show but steps in a full paint tray early in Day I.

Blind Ambition: Kia's window treatment plan is a fiasco: The blinds must be dismantled, hand-numbered (there are more than 150 of them), covered with spray adhesive, and attached to a piece of fabric. Each slat is then supposed to be cut apart and restrung so that either the fabric side or copper side is exposed. Midway through Day 2, Kia's male homeowner has only completed 1½ blinds, and the finished product looks horrible; he tells Paige, "If I were in charge, she [Kia] wouldn't get away with this." Paige tries to convince Kia to consider alternatives. Kia states that "there's no other plan!" In the end, the room doesn't have any window coverings.

Wise Words: Frank encourages his male homeowner while they're stuffing pillows by saying, "Become one with your batting."

Mirror Image: Paige asks whether Kia expects the homeowners to be able to see themselves in the CD "mirror" Kia designed. Kia and Paige debate the reflectiveness of the CDs until Kia finally looks at herself in a CD and says, "I'm a little distorted and very prismed, but I can see myself clearly." Paige doesn't buy it but helps with the project anyway.

Quotable Quote: During Designer Chat Frank tells Paige, "Romance doesn't have to be, like, socko-wow leather and lace."

Frank's Room: ☺ 😐 ☹
Kia's Room: ☺ 😐 ☹

San Diego: Duenda Road

Cast: Paige, Frank, Vern, Amy Wynn

The Rooms: Frank adds romance to a bedroom by painting the walls soft green, building a canopy frame out of molding strips, hanging a gauzy canopy from the ceiling, and revamping an existing dresser. Vern updates a living room by painting the walls with two tones of soft green, surrounding the existing fireplace with slate tiles, painting the existing furniture a third shade of green, hanging glass vases on the wall, installing green chenille draperies, and creating a new entertainment center.

Aquatic Antics: Most of the B-roll footage for the episode is the cast hanging out at SeaWorld. Frank kisses a dolphin, Paige talks to killer whales, Vern rides a dolphin, and Amy Wynn has all sorts of adorable escapades with a seal and a sea otter.

Quotable Frank: Frank-isms abound in this episode. Some highlights: "You don't have to strangle the roller, Mary. The roller is your friend, Mary." When a homeowner says that Frank's body is in the way of something the homeowner needs to see, Frank retorts, "My body's in the way of the entire wall!" Frank also accidentally calls his female homeowner "babe," only to realize the slip (and apologize for it) a few moments later.

Confession Time: Amy Wynn confides to the camera, "It's so hard getting used to all these different people's houses; you have no idea!"

International Flair: When Frank tells Paige that something is merely a suggestion, she replies, "Oh, kind of like a stoplight in Italy?"

Girl Time: Amy Wynn gushes about the function of the furniture piece she's building by saying, "Oh my God, shoe storage! I love it!"

Double Duty: Vern and his male homeowner joke that the wall vases can hold flowers or be beer dispensers.

Wise Words: During Designer Chat, Paige tells Vern, "You can't spend money to buy time."

Notable: Check out the end credits to see Paige and Frank demonstrate the "nonstop action" of *Trading Spaces*.

Frank's Room: ☺ ☺ ☹
Vern's Room: ☺ ☺ ☹

Los Angeles: Murrietta Avenue

Cast: Paige, Genevieve, Laurie, Amy Wynn

The Rooms: Gen gives a bland living/dining room a 1940s L.A. twist by painting the walls dark red, painting the trim bright white, adding white crown molding, and hanging draperies featuring a palm frond print. Gen also designs lighted display shelves, frames book illustrations of 1940s L.A., reupholsters the dining room chairs with more palm frond fabrics, and hangs a new period light fixture. Laurie creates a warm and comfortable living room by painting the walls butter yellow, with bands of golden camel and cream near the top of the walls. She installs built-in wall cabinets to house electronic equipment and "hideaway dog beds," lays a large khaki area rug, paints the fireplace white, slipcovers the sofa, and adds two green chenille chairs.

Ouch!: During the Opener, Gen and Amy Wynn watch as a tattoo artist inks the *Trading Spaces* logo onto Laurie's bicep.

Yucky Moment: As Gen cleans off a cluttered entertainment center shelf, she encounters the cremated remains of two dogs, stored in boxes with little dog statues on top of them. She's a little ooked out.

Girl Fight?: Gen jokingly contrasts her design style with Laurie's, claiming Laurie always manages to delegate tasks.

Gen then assumes a Southern accent and says, "Y'all, it's time to paint." Yet somehow, Gen still gets stuck doing the painting.

Musical Moment: Paige dances and spray-paints dining chairs while Gen's male homeowner plays polka music on the accordion.

Musical Moment, Part 2: Gen's male homeowner is a semicelebrity. He plays guitar and has toured with Alice Cooper, Slash, Guns N' Roses, and Carole King. (One of these things is not like the other...)

Musical Moment, Part 3: Slash (who's good friends with Gen's homeowner and a *Trading Spaces* fan) hangs out with Gen and the homeowner in Sewing World. Gen tells Slash to sit down and learn to sew too. He does.

Southern Charm: Laurie finds out on Day 2 that the carpet she ordered won't arrive for two more days. She and Paige go shopping and find a carpet Laurie likes. When Laurie asks the very nice carpet salesman (who happens to be friends with Gen's male homeowner, whose room Laurie is redoing) if the carpet is in her price range (she can only spend $45), he does some quick calculations with a calculator and says, "We're gonna make it in your price range." Laurie hugs him.

Notable: The end credits feature a long shot of *everyone* (and we mean everyone) doing a kick line.

Gen's Room: ☺ ☺ ☹
Laurie's Room: ☺ ☺ ☹

Las Vegas: Carlsbad Caverns

Cast: Paige, Hildi, Doug, Amy Wynn

The Rooms: To redecorate a living room, Hildi draws inspiration from a print she bought in London. She paints the walls dark red, paints the ceiling blue with light purple glaze, adds six red columns throughout the room, lays checkerboard vinyl flooring in two shades of orange, hangs deep red draperies, and adds slipcovers, upholstery, and pillows in every shade of the rainbow. Doug gets "Dirty" in a bedroom by covering the walls in dark brown Venetian plaster; he paints the ceiling peach, hangs bright blue draperies, sews pillows and bedding in various blue fabrics, installs crown molding, builds a large round white armoire, and creates a four-poster look around the existing bed with four alleged stripper poles.

Happy Couple?: During the Opener, Hildi and Doug go to a drive-through wedding chapel where Amy Wynn officiates. After Amy Wynn ominously says, "You are wed," Hildi and Doug kiss. Hildi pulls away and says, "Stop opening your mouth!" Doug looks coyly into the camera and shrugs his shoulders.

Thread-Bare: On the morning of Day 2, Hildi discovers that the fabric she shipped isn't going to arrive in time. She goes speed-shopping for fabric and must frantically sew everything in one afternoon.

Take That!: When Doug's male homeowner complains about painting the ceiling peach, Doug harasses him by asking what color the carpet is in his house. The carpet is a disgusting pink, so Doug tells the homeowner that because of his crappy carpet color he doesn't get a say in color choices.

Navel Alert!: No, not Paige. This time it's Amy Wynn showing her navel—for a long time while installing Doug's stripper poles.

Notable: The Reveals for this episode originally aired live.

Fame Game: Vegas celebs aplenty in this episode! Using a drill, Penn & Teller perform a card trick for Amy Wynn; Robin Leach presents Doug and his team with champagne and compliments them on upping the style in their homes;

Rita Rudner does the splits; and an Elvis impersonator helps Doug hang valances while singing "Amazing Paint." Only in Vegas, baby, only in Vegas.

Hildi's Room: ☺ ☺ ☹
Doug's Room: ☺ ☺ ☹

General Index : Trading Spaces Color

Use the following index as your handy guide to locating the topics, tools, looks, styles, and designers you're looking for. Jump in!

A-B

Accent colors, 127–128, 141
Accessories, 29, 113, 155
Acrylic sheets, 127, 130
Appliqué, 25, 85, 88
Armoire, 74, 119, 147
Artwork
  abstract, 35, 53, 77
  creative ideas, 26, 49, 63, 77, 123
  etchings, 26
  framed fabric, 47
  guitars, 127
  painted toenail, 65, 66
  paisley sculpture, 140
  photos, 79, 101
  portraits, 25
  snowboards, 59
  stalks of wheat, 74
Beads/bangles, 40, 99, 139
Beds
  canopies, 33–34, 37, 148, 149
  child's, 37
  creative ideas, 37
  daybed/settee, 115
  swags, 33, 147, 148
  swinging, 93
Bedspreads. See Linens
Bench
  bedroom, 107

coffee/end tables, 79
  kneeling, 93
  reupholstering basics, 110
  slipcover, 59
Black
  accents, 67, 128, 135, 139
  black/white, 79, 81, 109
  furniture, 40, 67, 79, 128, 138
  shading, 27
Borders, 93, 96, 139
Brushes/rollers, 36
Buttons, covered, 73, 76

C-D

Cabinets, painted
  kitchen, 19–20
  painting techniques, 22
Canopy
  creative ideas, 149
  making a, 148
  mosquito netting, 33–34
  PVC frame, 37
Ceilings
  cathedral, 103
  color, 41
  creative ideas, 103
  fabric, 99
  high, 40, 73, 107, 147
  metallic, 157

mirrors, 17
  painting techniques, 36
  wood, 155
Chair, painted, 15
Changeable color elements, 141
Chevreul's Laws, 99
Classic
  color combinations, 109
  stripes, 121
  style, 119
Color
  terminology, 27
  wheel, 21, 27, 95, 109
Columns, 53, 94
Complementary colors, 27, 95
Computer/desk, 128
Contrasting color, 95
Country style, 133–134
Curtains. See window treatments
Designers
  Doug, 19–21, 65–67, 73–74, 85–87
  Edward, 59–61, 127–128, 139–140
  Frank, 25–26, 147
  Gen, 33–35, 45–47, 99–101, 133–134
  Hildi, 13–15, 53–54
  Kia, 93–95, 113–115
  Laurie, 107–109

Vern, 39–40, 79–80, 115, 119–121, 151–155
Distressing technique, 22
Divider wall, 85, 139
Dog bed, 33
Dramatic look, 15, 25–26, 53–54, 59–61

E-F

Elegant style, 111
Entertainment center
  alcove, 80
  armoire, 119, 147
  faux pie safe, 134
  plywood boxes, 13
  wood, 153
Exotic style, 93–95, 97, 99–101
Fabrics
  bargain shopping, 75
  ceiling draperies, 99
  framed artwork, 47
  paisley, 139–140
  retro, 33
  silk, 93
  tie-dye, 65
  on walls, 73, 76, 80
Fireplace, 25, 65, 107, 115
Flashing, 62
Flexibility, 7, 15
Floor treatments
  carpet tile, 57
  ceramic tile, 120
  homemade rug, 85
  laying tile, 56
  linoleum/vinyl tile, 53, 56, 57
  stripes, 123
  wood, 155
Flowers/plants
  arranging, 102
  Birds-of-paradise, 19, 61
  fresh, 67, 83
  silk, 67
  tropical palm, 33
Funky style, 16, 53–54, 59–61
Furniture
  makeovers, 137
  painting techniques, 22

Project Index
Find the perfect decorating project fast and easy.

A-F

Acrylic sheets, 130
Appliqué pillows, 88
Borders, 96
Brushes/rollers, 36
Button covering, 76
Canopies, 148
Distressing furniture/cabinets, 22
Flashing strips, 62
Flower arranging, 102

H-R

Headboards, 82
Hook-and-loop use, 82
Lamps, 16
Metallic leafing, 156
Opaque projector, 28
Padding arms, 68
Painting furniture/cabinets, 22
Reupholstering a bench, 110
Rod pocket panels, 48

S-W

Screens, 136
Sewing pillows, 142
Sink skirt, 82
Slipcover measuring, 68
Stripes, 42, 122
Tile laying basics, 56
Upholstering walls, 76
Walls/ceiling painting basics, 36
Window topper, 82
Window treatment measuring, 116

G-H-I

Geometric style, 39, 85–86, 89
Hardware, 21, 33, 40, 134, 139
Hat box display, 25
Headboards
  grass-cloth, 33
  grid-style, 107
  molding strips, 147
  padded, 25
  paisley slipcover, 140
  stripes, 123
  using hook-and-loop tape, 82
Hollywood style, 79–81
Hook-and-loop tape, 80, 82
Inspirational sources, 15, 29, 66
International themes
  Arabia, 99–101
  Asia, 45–47
  Bahamas, 19–21
  Brazil, 65–67
  creative ideas, 97
  India, 93–95
  Polynesia, 33–35

L-M

Lamps
  lava, 59
  making, 16
  traditional, 134
Lampshades
  glass, 127
  gold pleated, 151
  lotus-blossom, 45
  paper, 35
  silk, 99
  tulle, 25
Leafing, metallic, 151, 155, 156
Lighting fixtures
  chandelier, 79, 109, 139, 151
  halogen pendent, 127
  puck lights, 61
  sconces, 40, 147
  spotlight, 21
Linens, 33, 74, 75, 87, 107, 111
Metallic
  accents, 99, 111, 151
  countertop, 61
  creative ideas, 157
  finishes, 60
  flashing, 61, 62
  furniture, 59, 61
  kitchen, 21, 157
  leafing, 151, 155, 156

Mirrors
  on ceiling, 17
  framed, 15, 34, 101, 115
  hiding TV, 139
  tiles, 57, 108
Moldings
  cabinet, 19, 22, 119
  canopy, 148
  chair rail, 73, 139
  faux crown, 103
  fireplace mantel, 115
  headboard, 147
  walls/ceilings, 155
Monochromatic colors, 27, 113, 115
Mood, 7, 47, 135
Mosquito netting, 33–34
Murals, 28

N-O-P

No-sew curtains, 48
Opaque projector, 28, 43
Ottoman, 45–46, 54, 68, 133
Paint basics
  brushes/rollers, 36, 42
  choosing hues, 47
  oil/latex, 35
  sheen, 35, 43, 95
  testing color, 87
Painting techniques
  creative ideas, 43
  distressing, 22
  furniture/cabinets, 22
  gauze look, 25
  primer, 36
  spray-paint, 15, 108
  stripes, 122
  walls/ceilings, 36
Paisley, 139–140
Pallet, wood
  display altar/bench, 93
  shelves, 94
Pillows
  appliquéd, 25, 85, 88
  bed, 140
  bolster, 47, 143
  creative ideas, 133, 143, 154
  neck roll, 127
  sewing basics, 142
  slipcovered, 13, 65

Q-R-S

Quiz
  color attitude, 8
  color type, 55

Record album display, 13
Repeating themes, 17
Romantic theme, 33–35, 147, 148
Screens, 15, 136, 151
Seating ideas, 117
Sewing techniques
  appliqué, 88
  pillows, 142
  rod pocket panels, 48
Shade, 27, 81
Sheen, 35, 43, 95, 133
Sink, fabric skirt, 82
Slipcovers
  chairs, 152
  couch, 54, 65, 121, 127
  creative ideas, 69
  measuring for ready made, 68
  padding arms, 68
Small spaces, 101, 127
Soothing look, 33–35, 39–40,
    45–46, 93–94
Spray paint techniques, 15, 108
Stained glass windows, 119
Stencils, 66, 103
Storage options
  armoire, 74
  baskets, 20
  under bed, 37
  below sink, 83
  cabinets, 54
  under coffee table, 79
  shelves, 74
Stripes
  basics, 121
  creative ideas, 123
  flashing strips, 61, 62
  free flowing, 15
  gold leaf, 99, 101
  horizontal, 40, 42, 99
  painting techniques, 122
  vertical, 119
  window treatment, 67

T-W

Tables
  coffee, 54, 79, 85, 99,
    121, 137, 155
  creative ideas, 23
  display, 15, 101
  glass, 59
  night, 109
Tabletop displays, 83
Terminology, color, 27
Tile
  ceramic, 57

  creative ideas, 57
  laying tiles, 56
  linoleum/vinyl, 53, 56
  mirror, 108
Traditional style, 107–109, 113–115
Tropical style, 19–21, 33–35
Upholstering techniques
  bench, 110
  padding arms, 68
  walls, 73, 76, 80, 82
Wainscoting, 73, 155
Wall treatments
  border, 93, 96, 139
  curtain panels, 80
  flashing strips, 61
  geometric ideas, 89
  mirror tile, 57
  painting techniques, 36, 43
  plywood squares, 39
  stencils, 66
  stripes, 40, 42, 119–121
  upholstered walls, 73, 76, 80, 82
  wood, 155
  wood-veneer wallpaper, 151, 152
Warming styles, 73–74,
    79–80, 85, 151
White
  accents, 65, 74, 115, 134
  black/white, 79, 81, 109
  Chevreul's Laws, 99
  elegance, 119
  romantic, 147
  tint, 27
Window treatments
  acrylic sheets, 127, 130
  baluster valance, 95
  creative ideas, 131
  hook-and-loop
    attachment, 82
  matchstick blinds, 33, 131
  measuring, 116
  no-sew curtains, 48
  panels, 67, 107, 133, 140, 154
  rod pocket panels, 15, 116
  sewing basics, 48
  sheers, 47, 94, 95, 147
  stained-glass panels, 127
  swags, 113
Wood, 155

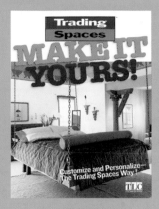
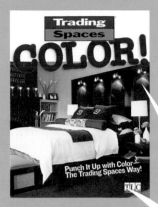